KU-497-232

CONTENTS

Also available
Bloomin' Rainforests · Cracking Coasts · Desperate Deserts ·
Earth-Shattering Earthquakes · Freaky Peaks · Monster Lakes · Odious
Oceans · Perishing Poles · Stormy Weather · Violent Volcanoes ·
Wild Islands

Horrible Geography Handbooks
Planet in Peril
Wicked Weather
Wild Animals

Specials
Intrepid Explorers
Horrible Geography of the World

Scholastic Children's Books,
Euston House, 24 Eversholt Street,
London, NW1 1DB, UK

A division of Scholastic Ltd
London ~ New York ~ Toronto ~ Sydney ~ Auckland
Mexico City ~ New Delhi ~ Hong Kong

First published in the UK by Scholastic Ltd, 2000
This edition published by Scholastic Ltd, 2008

Text copyright © Anita Ganeri, 2000
Illustrations copyright © Mike Phillips, 2000, 2008

ISBN 978 0439 94456 4

All rights reserved

Printed and bound by CPI Group (UK) Ltd, Croydon, CR0 4YY

13 15 17 19 20 18 16 14 12

The right of Anita Ganeri and Mike Phillips to be identified as the author and illustrator of this
work respectively has been asserted by them in accordance with the Copyright, Designs and
Patents Act, 1988.

WAT-ER PAIN IN THE NECK!

HORRIBLE GEOGRAPHY

RAGING RIVERS

ANITA GANERI ILLUSTRATED BY MIKE PHILLIPS

SCHOLASTIC

INTRODUCTION

Geography is full of horrible surprises. Take learning about rotten rivers, for a start. One minute, you're sitting in your nice, warm classroom, nodding happily off to sleep while your geography teacher's voice goes on and on and on...

> TODAY'S LESSON IS ALL ABOUT FLUVIAL BEDLOADS.* OPEN YOUR BOOKS AT PAGE BLAH, BLAH, BLAH...

* That's the tricky technical term for a river's sandy bottom.

You close your eyes and start to dream... You're sitting on a grassy riverbank, a long, cold drink in one hand, a fishing rod in the other. Lovely. The sun is shining, the birds are singing, geography doesn't seem so boring after all. Bliss.

Suddenly, your dream turns nasty. Really nasty. Now you're standing in the pouring rain, up to your knees in muddy water. Feeling like a drowned rat. What a nightmare. Yes, your teacher's taken you on a ghastly geography field trip. And it's HORRIBLE.

So horrible that you're glad to wake up and find yourself back in your geography lesson again. It may be boring but at least it's dry.

But not all geography is dismally damp and uncomfortable. Some bits are horribly exciting and interesting. Try this simple experiment. Smile sweetly at your mum, dad or guardian and tell them you're off for a bath. Don't wait for a reply, they'll be too shocked to speak. Go into the bathroom and turn the taps on full. How long does it take the bath to fill up? About ten minutes? Now try to imagine 200 MILLION bath taps turned on full. This is how much water it takes to fill the awesome Amazon, the biggest river on

Earth. (Back in your bathroom, pull out the plug, flap your towel around, and pretend you've had a good, long soak. Your grown-up will be ever so impressed.)

And that's what this book is all about. Long enough to stretch right around the world, strong enough to carve out mile-deep valleys, angry enough to flood a whole town, with wicked waterfalls as tall as the Eiffel Tower, rushing rivers are all the rage. In *Raging Rivers*, you can…

* explore the world's greatest rivers with Travis, your intrepid tour guide.

* take the plunge over the world's highest waterfalls.

* catch and cook a piranha for lunch (mind your fingers).

- learn how to survive in a flood (against all the odds).

This is geography like never before. And it certainly isn't boring. All you have to do is keep turning the pages. You don't even need to get wet. Unless, of course, you drop your book in the bath…

WILD WEST BY RIVER

The amazing adventures of Lewis and Clark
Washington DC, USA, 1803

The two young men summoned to President Thomas Jefferson's office shivered slightly, although the room was warm. They had just been handed the most important mission of their lives – to lead the first ever official expedition across the wild west of America to find a river route to the Pacific Ocean.

Jefferson's idea was to open up these lands for trade and settlement, and to make America richer and more powerful than ever before. There was just one problem. No one had explored these vast lands before. No one knew what dangers lay ahead for them or if they would ever make it back home. It was enough to make anyone shiver. President Jefferson shook their hands and wished them goodbye and good luck. He didn't care what other people said. He was sure that he'd found the right men for the job.

The two men in question were dashing Captain Meriwether Lewis, the President's trusty private secretary, and Lewis's old friend, Lieutenant William Clark. They were young, strong, brave and handsome. They'd need to be all of these things (OK, so good looks weren't that important).

It was going to be a long and rocky road. Lewis and Clark put their heads together and soon they'd hatched a daring plan. They would travel up the Missouri River, as far as they could go, cross the Rocky Mountains, then follow the Columbia River to the Pacific. Simple!

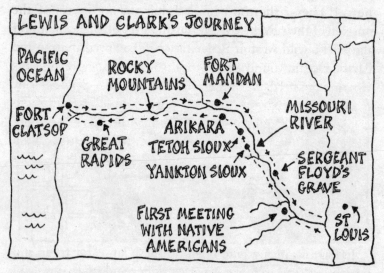

They spent the winter preparing for the expedition. They were not travelling alone. With them went a group of 43 men, mostly soldiers, grandly named the Corps of Discovery. They also took six tonnes of food (when this ran out, they'd have to hunt for more), weapons, medicines, scientific equipment and gifts for the local people.

These were loaded into three sturdy boats – one barge and two canoes. These were crucial. Without good boats, it was sink or swim.

At last, on Monday 14 May, 1804, everything was ready. A single shot was fired to signal the off and the expedition headed out of the town of St Louis on the banks of the Missouri. It would be two and a half years before they would see home again. From St Louis, they followed the mighty Missouri as it wound westward, through rolling green plains where huge herds of buffalo roamed. For five months, they made steady progress. Canoeing upriver, watching the world go by, was really quite pleasant. The only flies in the ointment were the swarms of mosquitoes constantly buzzing around their heads. Very irritating.

In October, they reached the land of the Mandan Indians. They were warmly welcomed, and decided to spend the winter there because the river would soon be covered in ice.

The winter of 1804–1805 was very long, very cold and very boring. On some days, temperatures plummeted to a teeth-chattering low of -40°C. The members of the expedition stayed snug and warm (but bored stiff) inside their log cabins. It was far, far too cold to risk setting foot outside those four walls.

By the following April, they were all glad to be on the move again. There was just one tiny hitch. So far, they'd been able to follow their route on some roughly-drawn charts but from here on the maps ran out. Completely. What lay ahead was utterly unknown territory. Without maps, Lewis and Clark had no idea what they were in for – whether or not they'd be hiking up mountains, wading through rivers or hacking their way through vegetation. There was just no knowing. And they could only hope that they were going in the right direction!

But plucky Lewis and Clark weren't worried. They hired a local Indian guide to help them out – someone who did know the lay of the land – and continued upriver to the Rocky Mountains. Now came the worst part of the journey. Crossing the mountains was a terrible ordeal. Their food ran short and at night the weather turned bitterly cold. All the men could do was grit their chattering teeth and keep plodding grimly on.

Their courage paid off. On the other side of the mountains lay wide open plains ... and the Columbia River. Finally, on 7 November 1805, they sailed down the river to its mouth in the sea. At last, they had reached the Pacific Ocean and their journey's end.

The following spring, they began their long journey home again, reaching St Louis on 23 September 1806. Lewis and Clark were given a hero's welcome. Everyone was glad to see them, especially as they'd been given up for dead. They'd covered some 7,000 kilometres, most of it by canoe. They'd been growled at by grizzly bears, rattled at by rattlesnakes, and riddled with frostbite, fear and starvation. Lewis had even been shot in the leg by someone who mistook him for a deer! It's true! Despite this, only one man in the team had died, probably from appendicitis. The expedition had been a raging triumph. True, their river route was not very practical. If you weren't a brave explorer, it was much too long and dangerous. (Many Americans did later follow in Lewis and Clark's footsteps, in search of new lands and trade, but they sensibly went overland by wagon.) Geographically, though, it was all a rip-roaring success. Lewis and Clark's expedition journals were crammed full of maps, sketches and notes about the rivers they'd sailed down and the people they'd met. (They kept notes about absolutely everything. That's the sort of thing geographers do.) Places and people that horrible geographers had never seen before.

GOING WITH THE FLOW

Of course, good old Lewis and Clark weren't the first people to realize just how horribly handy rivers can be. They used rivers to get them from A to B. But people have also been drinking them, washing in them, fishing in them and generally messing about in them for years and years.

The Romans even built a city on one. According to legend, the city of Rome was built by two brothers called Romulus and Remus. They were identical twins. Their mum was the priestess Rhea Silvia. Their dad was Mars, the god of war. So far, so good. The one bad apple in their happy family was their wicked great-uncle, cranky King Amulius.

* That's Roman for cheese.

Great-uncle Amulius was worried sick that one day when the twins were older they'd try to seize his throne. So he shoved them in a basket and chucked them into the raging River Tiber. As well as saving his royal skin, it would save him a fortune in birthday presents.

The twins drifted downstream and came to a stop at the bottom of the Palatine Hill. There a she-wolf found them. But instead of wolfing them down for lunch, she took them home and brought them up to be nice, well-behaved, er, wolves.

Later, they moved in with a kindly shepherd. (They had to promise not to chase the sheep.) But they never forgot their happy wolfhoods and decided to build their old wolf-mum a splendid city on the spot where she'd found them. For her retirement.

Building began. But things soon went horribly wrong. Romulus and Remus fell out big-time, over the height of a wall! You see, Romulus built the wall to defend the city from attack. But Remus said it was useless, way too low to stop anyone. And to prove his point, he jumped over it.

Romulus was furious. Did the twins make up? Nope, they did not. Romulus pulled out his sword and killed Remus. Then he named the riverbank city after himself.

So, if you believe your legends, Rome was built next to the River Tiber by a pair of twins brought up by a kindly wolf. Sounds reasonable.

Teacher teaser

Outwit your teacher with this Roman river talk:

OOH MISS, LOOK! JENKINS HAS DESCENDED INTO THE FLUVIAL FLOW!

What has Jenkins done?

Answer: Roughly translated, this means "Ooh Miss, look! Jenkins has fallen in the river." "Fluvial" is the posh name for anything to do with rivers. It comes from Latin, the old language of the river-loving Romans.

What on Earth is a raging river?

Some bits of geography are horribly difficult to understand. Don't worry, you can leave those bits out. This book is about the other bits, the bits that will turn you into a genius geographer without any effort at all. Take raging rivers, for instance. Your teacher may try to bamboozle you with all sorts of boring and baffling facts about rivers. Take no notice. It's just your teacher trying to make himself or herself feel important. Pathetic, eh! The horrible truth is that a river is a stream of freshwater (that means it's not salty like the sea) that flows across the land. Simple!

Water on the brain

You might think that yummy chocolate milkshake is the most useful and precious liquid on Earth. But you'd be wrong – dead wrong. While you could go for weeks without a milkshake, without water to drink, you'd be dead as a dinosaur in a few days. And where does most of this water come from? From raging rivers, of course. Rivers might only make up one per cent of the Earth's water, but that one per cent is fresh water which, when it's been cleaned, we can drink.

ARE YOU SURE THIS WATER'S BEEN CLEANED?

The first person to study water seriously (well, it takes all sorts) was British scientist, Henry Cavendish (1731-1810). Henry was born in Nice, France but spent most of his life in

London. Now nice Henry was a bit of a loner. He lived with his dad, until his dad died, and didn't go out very much. Well, you wouldn't either if you'd had Henry's dire dress sense. His favourite outfit was a hopelessly unfashionable purple suit, with a frilly collar and matching cuffs, topped off by a threadbare three-cornered hat. It looked frightful. No wonder Henry didn't have many friends. He certainly didn't have a girlfriend. In fact, he wouldn't even allow girls to set foot in his house. He thought they were a bad influence.

Luckily, Henry had one saving grace. He was absolutely brilliant at chemistry. He spent most of his time in his house, doing chaotic chemistry experiments. (He much preferred chemistry to people. After all, test tubes couldn't talk back.)

Anyway, when lucky Henry was 40 years old, he inherited a million pounds. He was rich! But did he let the money go to his head? Oh no. Did he blow all his cash on fine wine, fancy clothes or exotic holidays? Nope, he did not. He continued to work as hard as ever and spent most of his lovely lolly on … guess what? You've got it, it went on yet more chemistry kits and chemistry books. And it was just as well for horrible geography that it did because not long afterwards Henry Cavendish made the most amazing discovery. One day, in his laboratory, he mixed up some hydrogen and oxygen gas in a jar and heated the mixture up. What do you think he saw?

The sides of the jar covered with soot?

The sides of the jar covered with water?

The sides of the jar covered with slime?

Answer: b) The sides of the jar were covered with water. What brainy Henry had discovered was that water is not made of one single substance (i.e. plain old water) as single-minded scientists thought. In fact, it's made up of two gases, hydrogen and oxygen. The reaction between the two created water vapour which condensed (turned into liquid water) when it touched the sides of the jar. Incredible. In chemists' code, freshwater is called H_2O. That means two hydrogen atoms and one oxygen atom joined together as a water molecule. And billions and billions of wonderful water molecules make up a raging river.

Today, someone like Henry might be called a horrible hydrologer. That's the posh name for a geographer who studies river water. And hooray Henry was frightfully posh. Both his grandfathers were frightfully posh dukes who left Henry pots of frightfully posh dosh!

Earth-shattering fact

But where on Earth does all this horrible H_2O come from? It can't all be made in chemistry jars. And how does it get into raging rivers? Here's an Earth-shattering fact for you to flow with. The water found in raging rivers has flowed millions and millions of times before. In the water cycle, it's recycled again and again. So the water flowing in the awesome Amazon may once have flowed through Ancient Rome. Mindboggling, eh? To see how the water cycle works, imagine you're one of hard-working Henry's marvellous molecules. (Better still, imagine your geography teacher as one.) OK, so you'll have to use your imagination!

You're about to go on a very long journey. Over the page there's a picture to show you the way. Are you ready to go with the flow?

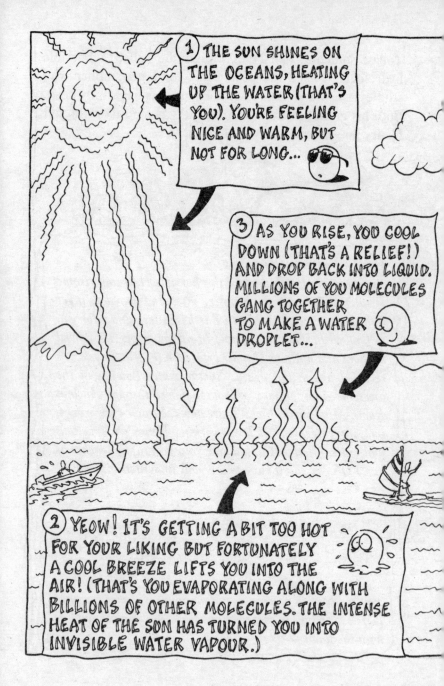

THEN MILLIONS OF DROPLETS GANG TOGETHER TO MAKE A CLOUD. THE SEA LOOKS A LONG WAY AWAY NOW.

5 INSIDE THE CLOUD THINGS ARE REALLY MOVING! OTHER MOLECULES ARE BASHING INTO YOU AND JOINING YOUR DROPLET UNTIL IT'S TOO HEAVY TO HANG AROUND. LOOK OUT! YOU'RE GOING FOR A LONG JOURNEY BACK TO EARTH. YEP, YOU'RE FALLING AS RAIN...

6 YOU MIGHT FALL INTO A RIVER WHICH CARRIES YOU TO THE SEA. YOU MIGHT FALL ON TO THE RIVER PLAIN AND TRICKLE INTO THE RIVER. YOU MIGHT SOAK STRAIGHT INTO THE GROUND. (OR YOU MIGHT FALL STRAIGHT INTO THE SEA.) BUT YOUR JOURNEY'S NOT OVER YET. NO WAY! IT'S ABOUT TO START ALL OVER AGAIN!

How on Earth do rivers flow?

1 Rivers always flow downhill. Which seems horribly obvious when you realize that they're dragged down by gravity. It's the same when you go downhill on your bike. You don't need to pedal – gravity does all the work. Gravity is a force which brings things down to Earth. It's what keeps your feet on the ground. It happens when a large object (the Earth) pulls a small object (the river or you on your bike) towards it.

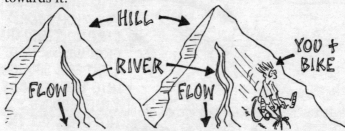

2 A river doesn't always flow at the same speed. It speeds up and slows down. This isn't because the river gets tired, it's because of a force called friction. You get friction when two objects try to push past each other and slow each other down, like when you're out shopping and get stuck in the

crowds. What's this got to do with rivers? Well, sometimes, friction between the river (Object No. 1) and its bed and banks (Object No. 2) slows the water down. A river flows fastest on the surface, near the middle, where friction is much weaker.

See how fast a river flows

What you need:

- a stopwatch
- a tape measure
- two sticks
- an orange
- a river

What you do:

a) Measure out a 10-metre stretch of river bank. Mark the start and end with the sticks.

10 METRES

b) Drop the orange into the water.

c) Time the orange as it flows downstream. (That's the direction the water's flowing in.)

d) Now for some boring maths. (You can skip this bit if it's too much like homework.) Remember how some bits of river flow faster than others? To work out an average speed for the whole river, you need to multiply your answer by 0.8. For example, if the orange travels 10 metres in 20 seconds, the flow speed is 0.5 metres per second. If you times this by 0.8, you get an average of 0.4 metres per second. (Experts use average speeds to work out things like how much water the river carries. But that's for another maths lesson!)

3 Rivers flow fastest down steep slopes, and you don't get much steeper than a waterfall. The Niagara River speeds up to 108 km/h as it plummets over Niagara Falls. That's about 16 times normal walking pace. Time to get your running shoes on!

WOW! A RUSHING, RAGING RIVER!

4 At any time, there's only enough water in all the world's rivers to keep them flowing for about two weeks. Without fresh supplies, they'd quickly dry up.

5 The Ancient Greeks had some funny ideas about what gets a river flowing. They knew all about the water cycle and all about rain. (A right bunch of know-alls they were.) But they didn't believe for a single minute that enough rain could fall to fill even one raging river.

They thought that the water must come from the sea, flowing into rivers through underground streams (and somehow losing its salty taste on the way).

6 In 1674, French lawyer, politician and part-time hydrologist Pierre Perrault measured the amount of rain falling in a year over the land drained by the River Seine.

What did he find? He worked out that there was enough rain to fill the Seine six times over and still have some left over for a quick wash. The clever-clogs Greeks had got it wrong!

7 Horrible geographers now know that water gets into rivers in four different ways. And they all start with rain. Here's Travis to guide you through them.

Some rain falls straight into the river. Simple!

Some rain falls on the ground. It runs downhill into small streams which flow together to make a river.

Some rain falls to the ground and freezes into glaciers. When the weather warms up, parts of the glaciers start to melt. This starts a stream, you can guess the rest!

ICE

Some rain falls and soaks into the ground. Boringly, it's called groundwater. Some of it flows straight into rivers. And as the rivers flow downstream, some rainwater gushes up as a spring.

UNDER GROUND

8 Luckily, rivers don't have to rely on groundwater for the whole of their water supply. Just as well. They'd be waiting a very long time. Groundwater flows very slowly. Very slowly indeed. This is what one scientist said about it:

A SNAIL MOVES FASTER THAN GROUNDWATER

BROOM! BROOM!

Another scientist, American John Mann, decided to see if this snaily tale was true. You can try his slimy experiment for yourself.

What you need:
- a tape measure
- a stopwatch
- a snail
- plenty of spare time on your hands

What you do:
a) Take the snail out into your garden.
b) Put it down on the path.
c) Time how long it takes the snail to trail along for a metre. (If you get bored waiting, cut the distance down.)

FINISH

What do you think happens:

a) The snail leads you up the garden path?

b) The snail moves at a snail's pace – obviously?

c) The snail moves faster than go-slow groundwater?

Answer: c) From his experiment, John Mann worked out that groundwater moves at only $\frac{1}{70}$th of a snail's pace. That's 70 times slower than a slowcoach snail! And who said doing science experiments wasn't boring!

Raging river record breakers: test your teacher

After all this flowing to and fro, you'll need a well-earned rest. Why not veg out on the sofa, put your feet up and leave the hard work to somebody else? Somebody like your geography teacher! Test their hydrological know-how with this quick quiz.

1 The Nile is the longest river on Earth. TRUE/FALSE?

2 The Amazon holds the most water. TRUE/FALSE?

3 The shortest river is D River. TRUE/FALSE?

4 The Rhine is the longest river in Europe. TRUE/FALSE?

5 Some rivers are usually dry. TRUE/FALSE?

6 Some rivers are completely frozen in winter. TRUE/FALSE?

Answers:

1 TRUE. The record-breaking Nile in Egypt is 6,695 kilometres long, making it officially the world's longest river. But it's a very close thing. The Amazon in South America is just 255 kilometres behind. Some horrible geographers see things differently. According to their measurements, the Amazon comes out longer. (Note: don't worry about these differences. Geographers are always falling out. You see, geography isn't an exact science, which means nobody knows anything for certain. So although geographers like to think they have an answer for everything, it isn't always the same answer!)

2 TRUE. The awesome Amazon carries more water than any other river on Earth, 60 times more than the Nile and one fifth of all river water on Earth. At its mouth, the Amazon empties 95,000 litres of water into the sea. EVERY SINGLE MINUTE! That's like emptying out 53 Olympic-sized swimming pools. Compared to this raging river, the Nile's a mere trickle.

3 TRUE. It's true that, at just 37 metres long, D River in Oregon, USA, is the world's shortest river. It flows from Devil's Lake into the Pacific Ocean.

4 FALSE. The vulgar Volga in Russia is 3,530 kilometres long and the longest river in Europe. The Rhine is only 1,320 kilometres long, less than half the Volga's length.

5 TRUE. Many desert rivers hardly ever have any water in them. Because there's so little rain in the desert, they're dry for much of the year. Other rivers are wet in winter and dry in summer.

6 TRUE. Every winter, the Ob-Irtysh River in snow-bound Siberia freezes along its whole length. The upper part of the river, high up in the mountains, stays frozen solid for five whole months. Brrr!

What your teacher's score means...

Allow two points for each correct answer. And no cheating...

10–12 points. Excellent. With such in-depth knowledge, your teacher will make a top hydrologist.

6–8 points. Not bad but the answers aren't quite flowing yet. If your teacher paid a bit more attention in class, he/she might just stay on course.

4 points and below. Oh dear! I'm sorry to say but your teacher's far too wet for this type of work. Better stick to teaching...

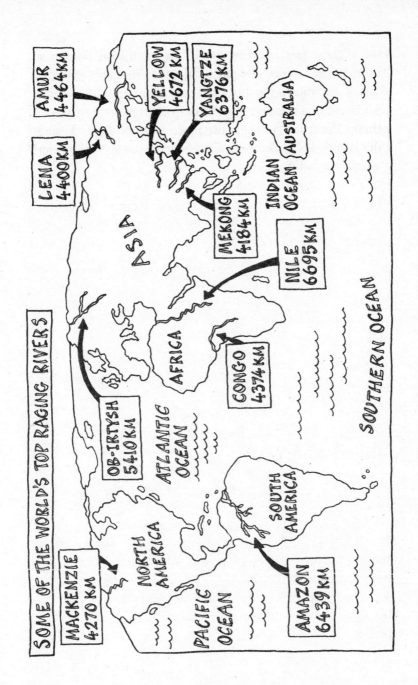

SOME OF THE WORLD'S TOP RAGING RIVERS

MACKENZIE 4270 KM

OB-IRTYSH 5410 KM

AMUR 4464 KM

LENA 4400 KM

YELLOW 4672 KM

YANGTZE 6376 KM

MEKONG 4184 KM

NILE 6695 KM

CONGO 4374 KM

AMAZON 6439 KM

NORTH AMERICA

SOUTH AMERICA

ASIA

AFRICA

AUSTRALIA

PACIFIC OCEAN

ATLANTIC OCEAN

INDIAN OCEAN

SOUTHERN OCEAN

Had a good rest? Feeling ready for anything? I hope so. You're going to need all your energy for the thrills and spills waiting for you in the next chapter. You're about to follow the course of a raging river all the way from its start until it reaches the sea. Are you ready to go with the flow? Time to put on your life jacket – just in case your canoe capsizes and you end up falling in!

RUNNING AWAY TO SEA

Rivers are a bit like people. They change as they get older. When they're young and just starting out in life, they rush about energetically and are full of get up and, er, flow. As they get older and more mature, they slow down and take things easier, meandering gently through middle age. Finally, old age catches up with them. As they near the sea and their journey's end, many get slow and sleepy, and a bit grumpy if you wake them up suddenly. Sound like anyone you know?

The river: a turbulent life story

Stage 1: Young river. At this youthful stage, the raging river's really flowing fast. It's a river in a hurry. And it's bursting with youth and energy. It's so strong it can carry horribly heavy rocks which scrape out the shape of its bed and banks.

Stage 2: Middle age. The river's starting to slow down now. It can't see the point of all that rushing about. It's dropped the rocks – they're much too heavy – but it still lugs along loads of mud and sand. And instead of smashing straight through obstacles, it sensibly meanders around them. Very grown up.

Stage 3: Old age. Now the river's so sluggish and slow it starts to drop off … zzzzzz, sorry, it starts to drop off all the mud and sand. Now and again it overflows its banks and floods but then it has to have a good, long rest until finally it flows into the sea.

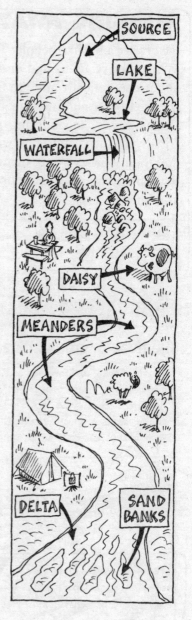

Stage 1: Young river

Source: OK, folks, good morning and welcome on board. My name's Travis and I'm your tour guide for today. And I don't mind telling you, you're in for a real treat. If you've got any questions, be sure to ask. As long as they're not too difficult!

So here we are at the source of the river — the place where our raging river begins and the start of our turbulent tour. The source might start off as rain falling on a mountain top or springing up from underground. (Water springs up out of the ground like this when the ground isn't "spongy" enough to absorb it.) Is everybody ready and comfy? It's all downhill from now on!

Drainage basin: Hello again. Wakey, wakey! If you look to your left and right, you'll see the river's drainage basin. Sorry, what was that question? Yes, the lad at the back. Oh, I see. No, it's not the thing your mum uses to drain veg or pasta for your tea! It's the land which supplies a river with water. Some rivers have horribly huge drainage basins. The Amazon's covers about 6.5 million square kilometres. That's twice as big as the whole of India. Gi-normous, I think you'll agree!

Tributary: See that little stream flowing in from the right? No, the right, sir, that's the left. Does anyone know what it's called? No? Oh well, never mind.

Geographers call it a tributary. No, madam, I don't know why they can't just say stream either. Believe me, it would make my life easier. But some tributaries are raging rivers in their own right. Take the Amazon again. It's got more than a thousand tributaries. One, the Parana, is among the longest rivers in the world.

Waterfall: And now for the most exciting part of our tour. I love this bit! Is everyone feeling brave? Plucky enough to take the plunge? I'm sorry, madam, it's much too late to turn back now. Even if you're feeling seasick... Hold on tight. You're about to have a jaw-dropping ride over a waterfall. A waterfall's where the river plummets over a step of hard rock (see page 64). Close your eyes if you're scared of heights. Here we goooooooo...

39

Stage 2: Middle age

Trunk: Wow! What a splash! We'll just stop here for a minute while I count up and make sure you're all here. Never mind, madam, it can happen to anyone. Now we're on the main bit of the river. Which has nothing to do with elephant's noses or trees. Though you could say that tributaries look a bit like branches growing from a tree trunk. If you were trying to be clever. Or poetic. The trunk is the bit that gives the river its name, like Nile, or Amazon, or, er, D. Get the idea? What's that, sir, you don't understand? I'll be along in a minute to explain.

Valley: See those high-rise slopes on either side? That means we're in a V-shaped river valley. It's been carved out of the rocks by the forceful flow of all that water (see page 57).

You get a splendid view from the top. But you'll need to take another tour for that, we've still got a long way to go. Don't worry, madam, we'll sort you a ticket out later. Put your purse away before it gets wet.

UP STREAM ← | → DOWN STREAM

Meander: Now I know that it seems we're going around in semicircles but rest assured, it's the river, not you, that's going round the bend! These great snaky S-shaped loops you can see in the river are called meanders.

Yes, sir? Good question — why are they called meanders? They're named after the meandering River Menderes in Turkey. No madam, we don't go there on this tour. To meander off course just for a moment, here's a quick diagram to explain how they work:

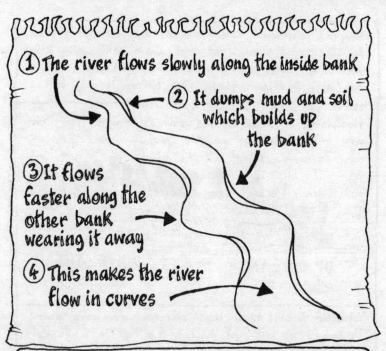

1. The river flows slowly along the inside bank

2. It dumps mud and soil which builds up the bank

3. It flows faster along the other bank wearing it away

4. This makes the river flow in curves

Ox-bow lake: Look at that lovely banana-shaped lake away to your left? No, not a banana-shaped cake, miss. We'll be having lunch in a very short time. That's right, madam, over there. It's called an ox-bow lake and it's where the river's cut straight across a loopy meander. Anyone want to take a photo? I would if I were you. It'll be no good leaving it till later - the lake may well have dried up by then.

Stage 3: Old age

Floodplain: See all that thick, gooey mud on your left and right? That's the river's floodplain. The mud means that the river's gone and flooded and tipped tonnes of goo all over the land (though other floodplains are covered in sand). It might not look very much, madam, but the mud's packed full of minerals which make brilliant plant food. Fruit and veg just love it. Which is why floodplains make fantastically fertile farms. And talking of food, it's time to stop for lunch!

Mouth: And here we are, folks! The mouth of the river and journey's end! Sadly, this is where we leave our river behind and watch it flow out into the sea. Here it drops the rest of its load of mud and sand. Some of this builds up into a delta (see page 71). Some of it's washed out to sea. And that's where you get off, folks! It's been great meeting you all, and I hope you've enjoyed the trip. Please be careful when leaving the boat. It might take a few moments to get your land legs back. And if you'd like to leave a small-ish tip, I've left a hat at the back. Thank you and see you soon!

Earth-shattering fact

Meanders may look bone idle, meandering along without a care in the world. But mind out if a meander's on the move near you. For years, the town of New Harmony in Indiana, USA, stood firmly on the banks of the Wabash River. The river meandered away meekly to the west. True, one loop was heading towards the town but at a snail's pace. There was nothing to worry about. Surely? Then one day in 1984 it started to flow faster, FOUR TIMES FASTER. At this rate, the town would soon be sunk as the river ate away at its foundations. Plans have been made to reroute the river and cut the earth-moving meander off. Will it work? The people of New Harmony are still waiting to see.

Teacher teaser

Next time a teacher asks you what you want to be when you grow up (boring!), pretend to think hard for a moment, then say:

Is that some sort of doctor who treats arms and legs?

The source of the problem

If your river tour hasn't left you soaked to the skin, think back to the place where it all started. Its source. There are three different types of sauce, sorry, source. No, not tomato sauce, cheese sauce and parsley sauce, or anything else you find lumps of in your school dinner. The *source* of a river is usually high up in mountains.

Can you match these three famous rivers to their sources? Go on – it could be the start of something really big.

Raging rivers to choose from:
1 River Ganges
2 River Amazon
3 River Rhine
Suitable sources to choose from:
a) a leaky lake
b) a glassy glacier
c) a springing mountain stream

45

Answers:

1 b) The source of the Ganges is a glacier in the Himalayas. They're very high mountains in Asia. In spring and summer, the tip of the glacier melts and starts off a stream which grows into the River Ganges. The Ganges flows right across India to the Bay of Bengal in the east. For many people, it's a holy river which fell from heaven and they worship it as a goddess. Below the glacier is a village called Gangotri. Thousands of pilgrims brave the wintery weather to travel here each year to worship the goddess and bathe in the icy river water. Brrr!

2 a) The awesome Amazon starts off as a trickle from a tiny lake high in the Andes mountains in Peru. The trickle flows into a stream called the Apurimac. That's the local word for "great speaker" because of the noise it makes as it roars downhill. From the lake, the Amazon flows right across South America (a staggering distance of 6,440 kilometres) to the Atlantic Ocean. Here it pours so much water into the sea that the sea doesn't start to get salty for another 300 kilometres.

3 a) and c) The raging Rhine begins life as two mountain streams flowing from the Swiss Alps. One glugs from the end of an icy glacier. The other leaks from a lake. The two join forces but they're not alone for long. Lots of other streams muscle in on their act. Then the river flows across Germany and Holland into the North Sea.

The sorry saga of the search for the Nile's source

You might think that finding the source of a river would be quite simple and straightforward. Surely even a horrible geographer couldn't miss a mountain stream? Especially if the river in question is incredibly long and famous, like the raging River Nile. Easy peasy, you might say. No problem. But you'd be wrong. Horribly wrong.

For hundreds of years, horrible geographers searched high and low for the source of the Nile. They knew that it must be somewhere in Africa, but Africa was a horribly huge country and most of it hadn't yet been explored. Several intrepid expeditions had set off to search for the source (including one sent by the nutty Roman emperor Nero). All of them returned in failure. Where on Earth did the Nile begin? It remained one of geography's best-kept secrets. Until one day in 1856, when two daring British explorers set off for Africa to really get to the source of the problem, once and for all. Their names were Richard Francis Burton (1821–1890) and John Hanning Speke (1827–1864).

Part I: The search begins
On 19 December 1856, Burton and Speke landed on the island of Zanzibar in the Indian Ocean. From here, they planned to head into Africa where the search would begin. They planned to venture into parts of Africa where no Europeans had ever set foot before.

But they didn't have time to worry. Stocking up for the journey took most of their time. They needed enough supplies to last the whole trip – they reckoned on it taking at least a year – and some porters to carry everything. (They were going to be much too busy exploring to carry anything themselves!) Among all the boxes and boxes of scientific instruments, books, tools and medicines, the two men allowed themselves some small luxuries, including a box of cigars, four sturdy umbrellas and a dozen bottles of brandy. For medicinal purposes, of course.

By June 1857, everything was ready and they finally set sail for Africa. Their route took them inland, then west to Lake Tanganyika. Then they would head north to the mountains to search for the secretive source. For eight hard months, they travelled on.

The heat was horrible, the flies were terrible, and the local people weren't always friendly. But Burton and Speke knew they could put up with almost anything if only they could find the source. Anything, that is, except each other.

The problem was that Burton and Speke were about as alike as chalk and cheese. As happy in each other's company as sausages and lumpy custard. You see, Burton was already a famous explorer, with several expeditions to Africa under his belt. He was brave and brilliant at everything, including

Secrets of the sand

Apart from towns and villages, many other deep secrets lie buried beneath the desert sand. Some have been there for years. Millions of years. Are you daring enough to go dinosaur hunting?

July 1923

The Daily Globe 🌍
The Gobi Desert, Mongolia

DINO GRAVEYARD FOUND IN GOBI

Ace American explorer, Roy Chapman Andrews, was today enjoying his new-found fame.

A team of experts led by Andrews has just unearthed a batch of fossilized dinosaur eggs – the first ever known. Andrews, who cuts a dashing figure in a wide-brimmed hat complete with feather, was understandably thrilled.

TICKLED PINK

"In spite of the pessimistic predictions before our start," he told our reporter, as he posed for a photograph, "we have opened a new world to science."

Dodging desert danger

He has every reason to be pleased. Very pleased. The 13 oblong-shaped eggs were found in one of the remotest parts of the Gobi Desert, a place as empty and unwelcoming as the surface of the moon. Andrews told us how the team had to travel hundreds of kilometres through the desert to reach them, braving sandstorms and bandit attacks on the way. Instead of camels, the team travelled in a fleet of converted Dodge motor cars, another expedition first.

DUNE BUGGY

Ancient egg-snatcher caught

Experts have been given the chance to examine the extraordinary eggs and believe they may have been laid some 80 million years ago. They were perfectly preserved by the bone-dry heat and soft desert sand, remaining hidden and untouched . . . until the American team found them.

SCRAMBLED EGGS

But that wasn't all Andrews discovered. More prehistoric surprises were to come. A further search revealed the bones of a small, toothless dinosaur near the nest, apparently caught red-handed as it tried to steal the eggs.

I'll be back, says Andrews

Before returning to his post at the American Museum of Natural History in New York, USA, Andrews plans to lead several more fossil-finding expeditions. "This is just the start," he said. "There may be hundreds more desert dinosaurs waiting to be discovered." And judging by what he's unearthed so far, things should get very exciting. Readers of the *Daily Globe* will be kept right up-to-date with the latest developments. With our exclusive coverage, it'll be just as if you were actually there.

RAIDERS OF THE LOST EGGS

Them dry bones

Dashing Roy C Andrews turned out to be right. There were loads more desert dinosaurs. He went on to find more dinosaur eggs and other fantastic fossils. His desert digs turned him into a star. The museum promoted him to director (not bad for someone who started out sweeping the floor) and he had a dinosaur named in his honour – *Protoceratops andrewsi*. (Why not try naming a dinosaur after your teacher?) He also wrote several bestselling books, including the gripping *In the Last Days of the Dinosaurs*.

Since then, scientists from all over the world have tried their luck in the dinosaur graveyard. And they haven't been disappointed. So far, they've dug up the bones of hundreds of dinosaurs, not to mention mammals and reptiles. The most exciting find of all was a dinosaur with feathers. It proved what scientists had thought all along – that early birds were descended from dinosaurs.

Desperate desert fact file

NAME: Gobi Desert

LOCATION: Central Asia (China and Mongolia)

SIZE: 1,040,000 sq km

TEMPERATURE: Hot summers up to 45°C; bitterly cold winters down to −40°C

RAINFALL: 50–100 mm a year

DESERT TYPE: Inland

DESERT DATA:

- In Mongolian, its name means "waterless place".
- It's the coldest desert in the world (apart from Antarctica).
- Most of it isn't sandy but bare rock and stones, with massive mountains on three sides.
- It's home to Bactrian camels (they're the ones with two humps).

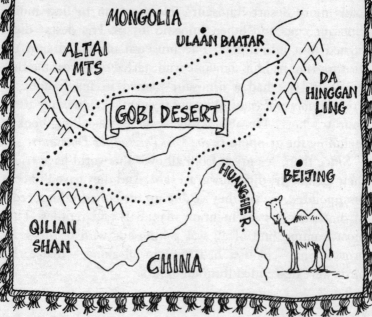

Designer deserts

Where do you find giant mushrooms and upside-down boats? And huge, stony tables? In the desperate desert, of course. They're all rocks carved into shapes by the weather.

Over millions of years, the weather wears the desperate desert landscape away. Geographically speaking, this wearing away's called erosion. Time to check out the main earth-movers-and-shapers involved:

• Horrible heat and cold. Baking hot days and freezing cold nights have an earth-shattering effect on the desert. By day, the rocks get hot and expand. At night, they shrink in the cold. Then the whole thing starts all over again. Day after day. Eventually, all this heating and cooling takes its toll. There's an ear-piercing BAAANNGG! as the rocks split apart at the seams and shatter into pieces.

- Rare rainfall. In the desert, it never rains but it pours. A sudden downpour can devastate the landscape. One minute it's dry as a bone, the next there's a flash flood racing towards you.

ONE MINUTE IT'S CHUCKING ROCKS AT ME, NOW IT'S TRYING TO DROWN ME!

(It's called a flash flood because it happens in a flash. Simple.) Flash floods carve out deep-sided gashes in the rocks, and sweep along tonnes of sand and boulders. When the rain stops, the water slows down and dumps its load. Then it evaporates. Just like that.

- Wild wind. Apart from stirring up sand dunes, the wind sends the grains of sand bouncing across the ground. Geographers call this saltation (which is Latin for leaping and jumping). Here's what happens:

1 The wind picks up a sand grain from the ground.

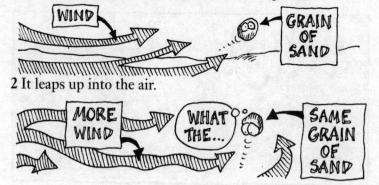

WIND

GRAIN OF SAND

2 It leaps up into the air.

MORE WIND

WHAT THE...

SAME GRAIN OF SAND

3 Then falls to the ground.

4 Then the whole thing starts again…

5 Sending the sand grain bouncing across the ground. Boingggg!

What on Earth has this got to do with erosion? Well, the wind blasts the sand at the desert rocks, wearing them away like a gigantic, and I mean gigantic, piece of sandpaper. But the sand can't bounce up very high. Instead it scrapes away at the rock close to the ground but can't reach up to the top. This goes on for years, until you're left with a rock shaped just like a mega-huge mushroom! Can you spot the difference?

Could you be a desert geomorphologist?

A geomorphologist (gee-ow-morf-ologist) is a horrible geographer who studies desert features. Well, it beats being called a boring old sand scientist. Fancy giving it a go when you leave school? (What d'you mean? You're not that desperate?) See if you've got what it takes with this quick-sand quiz.

1 An *erg* is a deadly desert disease. TRUE/FALSE
2 A *reg* is a one-humped camel. TRUE/FALSE
3 A *wadi* is a dried-up desert river. TRUE/FALSE
4 A *mesa* is a type of mountain. TRUE/FALSE
5 A *feche feche* is a fierce desert wind. TRUE/FALSE
6 A *playa* is a salty lake. TRUE/FALSE

Answers: 1 False. You're thinking of a l-erg-y. Geddit? *Erg* is the Arabic word for a vast sand sea covered in shifting sand dunes. Remember the lonely old Empty Quarter in the Arabian Desert? It's an enormous *erg*. **2** False. That's a dromedary – you're not even close! Though it's quite a cool name for a camel. *Reg* is the Arabic word for a stony, pebbly desert. It looks a bit like an old-fashioned cobbled street. **3** True. It's a deep gash or valley gouged out by a flash flood. A *wadi* can be dry for years and years, until a heavy downpour fills it with rain. Then you get a rare desert river.

"WADI'S" GOING ON HERE!

4 True. Geographically speaking, a *mesa* is a type of flat-topped mountain. It's left sticking up when the land all around it has been eroded away.

It also happens to be the Spanish word for table. But never mind knives and forks or table cloths. Some *mesas* are so enormous, you could fit a whole village on the table top. **5** False. *Feche feche* is actually very soft sand with a deceptively hard crust on top. It can measure just a few metres across or carry on for several kilometres. To be avoided at all costs, especially if you're in a car. Chances are it'll get you horribly bogged down. **6** True. Usually a *playa*'s dry as a bone but it fills up with water after heavy rain. When the water dries up in the sun, it leaves a layer of sun-baked salt behind. *Playas* are the flattest places on Earth. Flat as pancakes. Which is great news for space shuttle pilots. How? Well, one large *playa* in California, USA, is used as a landing site for the space shuttle. Cosmic.

OK. You've been walking for days and days. You've seen enough sand dunes and mushroom rocks to last you a lifetime but you haven't yet met a living thing – plant, animal or human. And you're beginning to feel a bit lonely. Desperate for company? Great news! Find out who or what is waiting to meet you as you drift over the page…

ONE HUMP OR TWO?

A desert may look deathly quiet and deserted but in geography things aren't always what they seem. Despite the horribly hostile conditions, desperate deserts are surprisingly lively and lived in. For hundreds of hardy plants and animals, deserts are home, sweet, home. So why don't they get all hot and bothered? Prepare for a sizzling surprise or two.

Keeping cool

If you despair at the thought of double geography, try spending a day in a desert. Don't fancy it? Talk about sticking your head in the sand! Luckily, there are dozens of daring creatures who call the desert home. But how on Earth do they do it? How do they cope with the heat and the drought? There are two main secrets to staying alive.

a) Finding water. All living things need water to survive. (And that includes you.) Otherwise their body bits can't function properly.

b) Staying cool. It's hot in the desert. Dead hot. Especially during the day. (That's why you don't actually see many animals. They're all fast asleep somewhere nice and cool. Zzzzzz.)

OK, so neither of these things are a problem in your geography classroom, with its leaky roof and its heating which never works. But in the desert they're a matter of life and death. Try this cool quiz to find out how some desert creatures cope.

Chill out quiz

1 What does a darkling beetle drink?
a) Rain.
b) Fog.
c) Cactus juice.

2 How does a sandgrouse fetch water for its chicks?
a) In its beak.
b) In a bucket.
c) In its feathers.

3 What does a ground squirrel use as a sunshade?
a) Its tail.

b) Its mate.

c) A camel.

4 How does the desert tortoise cool down?
a) It stays inside its shell.
b) It pees on its back legs.
c) It rubs spit on its head.

5 What does a fennec fox use its ears for?

a) Radiators.

b) Fans.

c) Er … hearing.

6 How do spadefoot toads stand the heat?

a) By living underwater.

b) By living under a cactus.

c) By sleeping underground.

7 How often do kangaroo rats have a drink?

a) Never.

b) Twice a year.

c) Once a month.

8 How do snakes cross the hot sand without getting burnt?

a) By hitching a lift on a camel.

b) By flying over the sand.

c) By slithering sideways.

Answers:

1 b) This beetle lives in the bone-dry Namib where it doesn't rain for months on end. So what does it drink if there isn't any water? Well, this ingenious insect drinks fog that rolls in off the sea. On misty nights, it stands on its head on a seaside sand dune, wiggling its back legs in the air. The fog condenses on to its body, then trickles down into its mouth. Brilliant, eh?

2 c) The sandgrouse lays its eggs in the scorching Saharan sand. The trouble is there's nothing for its thirsty chicks to drink. So the male sandgrouse flies off to an oasis and dives into the water. His feathers are specially designed to soak up water like a sponge. Back home, the chicks simply suck his feathers to get at the water. Simple. The sandgrouse is a doting dad – fetching the water often means a round trip of 100 kilometres or more.

3 a) The Kalahari ground squirrel uses its big, bushy tail as a parasol. It holds it over its baking body, at a jaunty angle, to give as much shade as it can.

4 b) When it gets really hot, the desert tortoise pees all over its back legs. Embarrassing but true! The pee dries in the sun and cools the toasted tortoise down.

5 a) The fennec fox uses its enormous ears to give off warmth, a bit like huge, furry radiators. Blood vessels flow across the surface of each ear, carrying warm blood with them. As air blows across them, it cools the blood (and the fox) down. Of course, the fox's ears also make brilliant, er, fox's ears, for listening out for juicy gerbils. Yum, yum!

6 c) Spadefoot toads spend nine months asleep in cool, underground burrows, lined with nice, damp slime. But at the first sign of rain, they leap into action. They hot-foot it to the nearest pool and lay their eggs in the water. Within two weeks, the eggs have hatched into tadpoles, the tadpoles have turned into frogs, and the frogs have hopped off into the desert. Then it's bedtime again.

7 a) Believe it or not, kangaroo rats never have a drink. They get all the water they need from seeds. Thirsty hawks and coyotes don't need to drink either. They simply gobble up a thirst-quenching kangaroo rat.

8 c) During the day, the acrobatic sidewinder rattlesnake has a clever way of getting across hot sand. It flips its body sideways and launches itself across the sand. In this way, its body only touches the sand for a few seconds and doesn't get burnt. Normally, though, sidewinders try to avoid the daytime heat and only get out and about at night when it's cool.

Snake, rattle and roll

Many desert snakes are poisonous. Deadly poisonous. To make matters worse, they're almost exactly the same colour as sand which makes them horribly hard to spot. Rattlesnakes have particularly poisonous reputations. But are they really as sinister as they seem? Some years ago we sent our *Daily Globe* reporter to find out more about them. And who better to ask than the world's leading expert on rattlesnakes, Laurence M Klauber (1883–1968), also known as Mr Rattlesnake. He spent 35 years studying, dissecting and writing about rattlesnakes. If he didn't know the answers no one would. Here's what he had to say.

When did you start getting interested in rattlesnakes?

When I was a boy in California. We didn't live too far from the desert, you see, where plenty of rattlesnakes live. I was really hooked on reptiles. But I was 40 years old before I started studying them seriously.

What did you do before that then?

I worked for an electrical company. I started off selling electric signs and ended up as president. I was really very lucky. But my real love was always reptiles.

So why did you leave?

I wanted to spend more time with the reptiles. So I became Curator of Reptiles at San Diego Zoo. They'd got several snakes they couldn't identify and they called me in to help. And I never left. It was a dream come true!

Do you ever take your work home?

Sure I do. I've got 35,000 rattlesnakes and assorted reptiles pickled in jars in my basement.

Gulp! And where did you get all those snakes from?

From the desert, mainly. If you're interested, a spring night's the ideal time to go. That's when the rattlesnakes are most active. Sacks are the best thing for catching them in.

Er, no, thanks, I'll give it a miss. And are rattlesnakes really deadly?

Not if you treat them nicely they're not. They'll only turn nasty if you get on their nerves. If you don't disturb them, they won't attack you. But if one starts rattling, turn around calmly and start to walk away. Whatever you do, keep your distance.

I'll take your word for it. Have you ever been bitten?

Er, yes, but only once or twice. I was lucky, it wasn't a particularly poisonous snake. The most dangerous rattlesnake is the eastern diamondback. Its markings make it tricky to spot and its bite can be fatal to humans.

Right. And what's all this about a rattle?

The rattle's made up of hollow, scaly rings at the tip of the rattlesnake's tail. When the snake shakes it, it makes a buzzing sound. Sounds quite eerie, in fact. It's meant to warn enemies to leave well alone. If they don't, the snake will strike. Also, you can tell individual rattlesnakes apart by the number of rings in their rattles.

Any tips for not getting rattled?

Yes. Wear a good pair of boots and a long pair of thick trousers, that's my advice. Then you might stand a chance. And if you're bitten, get yourself along to a doctor fast. Oh dear, are you feeling all right?

Earth-shattering fact

Forget rattlesnake-proof trousers. The deadliest creature in the desperate desert is the desert locust. Alone, these little fellows look small and harmless (one could perch happily on your thumb). But they never travel alone. These unstoppable insects fly around in swarms up to ONE THOUSAND MILLION strong. And they're horribly hungry! They devastate farmers' fields, devouring every plant in sight. What a swarm can guzzle in ONE DAY would feed 500 people for a year. Farmers have tried spraying them with super-strong insecticides but nothing seems to spoil their awesome appetites.

Design a desert-creature competition

Think you could do better? Why not enter our hot new competition to design the perfect desert animal? The fabulous first prize is an unforgettable camel safari through the record-breaking Sahara Desert. (Can I come with you?) Don't forget, you need to come up with a creature that can cope with baking heat, freezing cold, sandstorms, dust and lack of water. So it needs to be pretty special. Any ideas yet? Here's a clue — there's one desert animal that would win first prize in any creature feature competition (as long as it wasn't a beauty contest). Its survival skills are second to none. Can you guess what it is? Give in? It's the amazingly adaptable ... camel, of course. Forget cats and dogs. Camels are my favourite animals. And here's my very own Camilla to model the latest in camel cool...

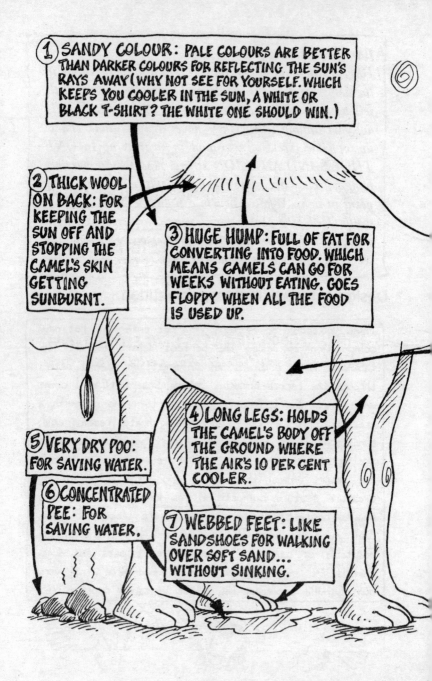

1. SANDY COLOUR: PALE COLOURS ARE BETTER THAN DARKER COLOURS FOR REFLECTING THE SUN'S RAYS AWAY (WHY NOT SEE FOR YOURSELF. WHICH KEEPS YOU COOLER IN THE SUN, A WHITE OR BLACK T-SHIRT? THE WHITE ONE SHOULD WIN.)

2. THICK WOOL ON BACK: FOR KEEPING THE SUN OFF AND STOPPING THE CAMEL'S SKIN GETTING SUNBURNT.

3. HUGE HUMP: FULL OF FAT FOR CONVERTING INTO FOOD. WHICH MEANS CAMELS CAN GO FOR WEEKS WITHOUT EATING. GOES FLOPPY WHEN ALL THE FOOD IS USED UP.

4. LONG LEGS: HOLDS THE CAMEL'S BODY OFF THE GROUND WHERE THE AIR'S 10 PER CENT COOLER.

5. VERY DRY POO: FOR SAVING WATER.

6. CONCENTRATED PEE: FOR SAVING WATER.

7. WEBBED FEET: LIKE SANDSHOES FOR WALKING OVER SOFT SAND... WITHOUT SINKING.

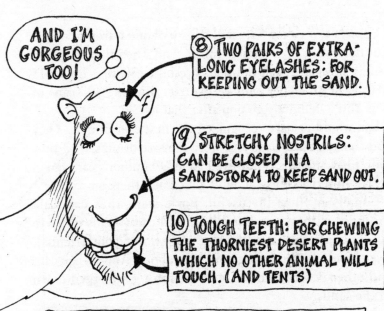

⑧ TWO PAIRS OF EXTRA-LONG EYELASHES: FOR KEEPING OUT THE SAND.

⑨ STRETCHY NOSTRILS: CAN BE CLOSED IN A SANDSTORM TO KEEP SAND OUT.

⑩ TOUGH TEETH: FOR CHEWING THE THORNIEST DESERT PLANTS WHICH NO OTHER ANIMAL WILL TOUCH. (AND TENTS)

⑪ THIN HAIR ON TUM: LETS HEAT ESCAPE FROM THE CAMEL'S BODY TO COOL THE CAMEL DOWN.

Some hump-backed facts about camels

1 Can't tell one camel from another? Simple – just count their humps. A one-humped camel is called a dromedary. It lives in Arabia, Asia and Africa. Two-humped camels are Bactrians. They come from the Gobi. They get through the freezing winter by growing a shaggy, woolly coat.

69

2 Camels can go for days and days without a drop to drink. But they work up a terrible thirst. And when they do get to water, they can guzzle down an awesome 130 litres in just 15 MINUTES! That would be like you drinking 400 cans of pop. You'd definitely go pop after that lot.

3 You wouldn't have recognized the first ever camels. They had short, stumpy legs and were the size of pigs. And they didn't have humps. They lived about 40 million years ago in North America (but you don't get camels there any more).

4 Camels are horribly useful. For a start, they can walk for miles without food or water. And carry loads of up to 100 kilograms (that's like you and two of your friends). Very handy for humping your tent about. And unlike cars and other desert vehicles, camels don't get bogged down in the sand.

5 Some desert people rely on camels for their living. They buy and sell them at camel markets (the white ones are worth the most). The more camels you have, the better off you are. Fewer than 20 is nothing to boast about. But 50 or more means you're rich. Camels also make brilliant wedding presents.

IT'S NOT ANOTHER TOASTER, IS IT?

6 And that's not all. People make tents and carpets from camel hair, and bags and rope from their hide. They even use camel pee to wash their hair. Apparently it leaves your hair nice and shiny and kills any irritating lice. Are you brave enough to give it a go?

7 Camel milk is crammed full of goodness and is rich in vital Vitamin C. (It's good for your teeth and bones. If you don't fancy a nice hot cup of camel milk before bedtime, you can also find it in fruit and veg.) You can either drink it straight, let it go off a bit or make it into yummy yoghurt. It tastes a bit like runny fudge. Fancy a spoonful?

FUDGE-FLAVOURED CAMEL YOGHURT RECIPE

Ingredients:
- some camel milk

Equipment:
- a large pan
- a bag made out of a goatskin
- a tripod made out of three sticks
- some rope

What you do:

1 Milk your camel. (Mind it doesn't kick you.)

2 Put the camel milk in the pan and heat it over the fire.

3 When it's warm but not boiling, pour it into the goatskin bag.

4 Hang the bag from the tripod, using the rope.

5 Give the bag a good shake. Repeat every few minutes for about two and a half hours until the mixture's thickened up a bit. (Warning: it will make your arm ache.)

6 Now tip it into bowls and serve it up to your friends. (If you dare…)

Horrible Health Warning
Camels aren't called "ships of the desert" for nothing. After an hour or two of sitting on a camel's back and swaying to and fro, you'll be feeling horribly seasick.

Desert plant dilemmas

Life's no picnic either for desert plants. Like animals, they need water to live. Without it, they'd shrivel up and die. In fact, they need water to make their food. Pretty vital, eh? Yet an amazing number of plucky plants live in the bone-dry desert. So how on Earth do they do it? It's a bloomin' miracle. Take the most famous desert plant of all, the skyscraping saguaro cactus...

WANTED

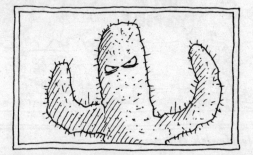

HAVE YOU SEEN THIS PLANT?

Name: SAGUARO CACTUS

Known haunts: Sonoran Desert, USA

Vital statistics: Height: 18 metres. Weight: 10 tonnes. Age: up to 200 years.

Distinguishing features:

● Thick stem: for storing up to eight tonnes of water.

● Groovy pleats: lets stem double in size to fit all that water in.

● Waxy skin: to seal moisture in.

● Sharp spines: large leaves leak loads of water into the air. Fine spines lose much less. They also shade the cacti from the sun. And see off creatures who fancy a nibble.

- Roots: shallow and branching for sucking up as much rain as possible as soon as it hits the ground.
- Elf owl: nests in a hole inside the cactus. If it's an elf owl, it must be a saguaro. (Though it's not strictly a distinguishing feature.)

Any known accomplices: About 2,000 suspects, including the barrel cactus, teddy bear cactus, beavertail cactus, old man cactus, hedgehog cactus, organ pipe cactus, to name a few.

Any known enemies: Ruthless cacti rustlers who go around stealing cacti from the desert without getting a permit. They cart them off and sell them to budding gardeners. Stolen saguaros can fetch around US $1,200 (£750) for a cactus 5 metres tall, with an extra $50 (£30) bonus for each extra arm. In Arizona, there's now a full-time cactus cop to round up the rustlers.

Warning! This plant is armed and dangerous. A very prickly character indeed. Do not go near it. Even if you're dying for a drink. Especially if you're dying for a drink. Its juice is horribly poisonous to humans.

If you spot a cactus in the Sahara, something's gone horribly wrong. Cacti only grow in the USA. So it's either a mirage (see page 102) or you're in the wrong desert. Oops!

Desperate desert fact file

NAME: Sonoran Desert

LOCATION: South-west USA and Mexico

SIZE: 310,000 sq km

TEMPERATURE: Hot summers from 41°C; cold winters to 3°C and below

RAINFALL: 50–250 mm a year

DESERT TYPE: High pressure

DESERT DATA:

• It's home to masses of wildlife, including pronghorn antelopes and mountain lions.

• It's prone to earthquakes because it lies close to the shaky San Andreas Fault, a colossal crack in the Earth.

• It's one of several North American deserts. You'll also find the Great Basin Desert, the Mojave Desert, the Painted Desert and the Chihuahuan Desert (yep, like those diddy dogs).

Bloomin' marvellous

Now, cacti may be the most famous plants in the desert but they're not the only ones. I've come across some marvellous bloomers on my travels. Here are some other ways in which these parched plants track down life-saving water. Ingenious, I think you'll agree.

One of the most down-to-earth desert plants is the marvellous mesquite bush. With roots an amazing 20 metres long, it can really get to the root of the problem. And the problem is finding water. Its roots reach down deep under the desert to suck up underground water. It's a bit like you slurping a drink through a 20-metre-long straw.

The cunning creosote bush does the opposite. Its tiny roots branch out far and wide to suck up dew and rain from all over the surface. Clever, eh?

The weird welwitschia of the Namib looks just like a giant turnip. At least, that's what it looked like to me. Except for the long, leathery leaves sticking out of the top. This peculiar plant only has two leaves but they can grow up to 3 metres long. They trail over the ground, getting terribly ragged and tattered at the edges. But they're also horribly helpful. They soak up fog blowing in off the sea and keep the wind-blown welwitschia well watered.

Last but not least, my own personal favourite. For most of the time, as you know, deserts look desperately dry and deserted. But in summer, when there's the best chance of some rain, it's a different story. Then the desert bursts into bloom. How? Well, there are billions of seeds buried under the ground. They've been there since the last time it rained, months or even years ago.

As soon as it rains, the seeds start to sprout. And in no time at all, the desert's decked out in fields of brilliantly coloured wildflowers, like desert daisies and dandelions. Now that's what I call bloomin' lovely.

ALL THIS TALK OF FOOD HAS MADE ME HUNGRY

BEFORE

AFTER

OOOH, PRETTY

DESERTED DESERT

BLOOMIN' DESERT

But how on Earth do these flowers pick the best time to bloom? The truth is that these secretive seeds have a very special coating. It contains a chemical which stops the seeds sprouting until there's plenty of rain. Enough, in fact, to soak into the ground and wash the coating off. It's just as well. If the seeds tried to grow during a light shower, they'd soon wither and die when the sun came out again.

And finally...

Speaking of secretive, spare a thought for the desperate devil's hole pupfish. Its only home is a tiny underground pool in the middle of the desert. The rest of its habitat has all dried up. So the poor old pupfish has NOWHERE ELSE TO GO. Put yourself in the penned-in pupfish's place. Imagine being stuck in your geography classroom for ever. Now that's a horrible thought.

DESPERATE DESERT LIVING

Desert living may be cool for camels. But what about human beings? Surely the desert's too hot for them to handle? Well, incredibly it isn't. Despite the desperately harsh conditions, a mind-boggling 650 million people, that's 13 per cent of the world's population, live in the deadly deserts. And they've been doing it for years and years. They've found ways of coping with the heat and finding water that would put you to shame. But don't be fooled into thinking it's easy for them. Life in the desert can be horribly hard. Are you ready to find out how they do it? Why not spend a day with Sandy and the San people of the Kalahari Desert in Africa...

MY NOTEBOOK
A DAY IN THE LIFE OF THE SAN
by Sandy

Hi, Sandy here. I'm here in the Kalahari, spending the day with the San people. It's such an honour to be here, I can't tell you. These are people who really know how to survive in the desert. They'll certainly be able to teach me a thing or two.

Dawn
It's dawn and time to get up and make a fire. It's pretty chilly in the desert first thing in the morning. Lucky I brought a blanket. There aren't any bathrooms in the desert, of course,

81

but a bush makes a good toilet. There's no water either, at least not to waste, so instead of a wash, the San rub red sand over their bodies. Actually, it works quite well. Breakfast is a couple of spoonfuls of porridge.

dirty → clean

NOTES:

To make a fire the traditional San way, you need to use a fire drill. No, not the sort where you hear a loud bell and file out into the playground. It's made of two long sticks. One stick has a hole in it which the other stick slots into. Then you twist the long stick around in your hands until you get a spark. Simple when you've had plenty of practice!

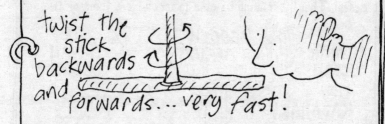

twist the stick backwards and forwards... very fast!

Early morning

After breakfast, the men set off hunting. They travel very light. All each hunter carries is a bag with his hunting spear, bow and arrows, digging stick (for finding water) and a fire drill (see Notes). I'm afraid I can't go with them this time but one of the hunters told me what happens. After walking for miles and miles through the desert, they finally track down an antelope. (There's some extraordinary wildlife in the Kalahari. Not just antelopes, but elephants and giraffes, too. It's finding them that's the tricky bit. Luckily, the San hunters know the desert like the back of their hands.)

bow
arrows
animal skin bag

When they track the antelope down, they fire. Their arrows are tipped with poison squeezed from a small but deadly beetle. The antelope doesn't stand a chance.

Back at the camp...
While the men are away, I'm off into the desert with the women and children to search for seeds and roots to eat. These are an important part of the San's daily diet. But it's hard work finding enough of them. I spend most of the time swigging water from my water bottle. The San women laugh at me. They don't need water bottles. When they're thirsty, they look for a small, dried-up plant sticking out of the sand. Goodness knows how they spot it. Looks just like a twig to me. Then it's time to start digging. It turns out that the twig thing actually belongs to a large, round tuber (a swollen plant stem). If you squeeze it, it drips with water. Very clever.

tuber

83

Any spare water is stored in empty ostrich egg shells which are sealed up and buried for later.

NOTES:
The San are experts at finding water. Here's how they make a traditional "sipwell":

1 They find a patch of damp ground and dig a deep hole.
2 Then they stick a hollow reed into the hole, like a drinking straw.
3 They fill the hole up, with the reed straw sticking out.
4 Gradually, water collects round the end of the straw.
5 When someone's thirsty, they simply slurp it up.

reed straw

SUCK
UP
water

Later that day
We get back to the camp just before the men. They arrive carrying the antelope. They have a really ingenious way of cooking it. First the men skin the antelope, then bury it in a hole in the hot sand. Then they light a fire in the hole and cover the whole thing with sand. When the meat's cooked, they cut it into strips. Brilliant. Then it's time for a feast! Everyone's hungry. Nothing goes to waste. Some of the meat is eaten straightaway. (And it's delicious, I must say.) Some is saved and

dried for winter. The antelope's skin is made into bags and clothes, and its bones are used for arrows. The San even eat the gristly bits in its ears. After all, it may be a while before they catch another one.

Sunset
After the feast, when we're all feeling full, the San sing songs and dance around the campfire until late into the night. They tell me that it's to thank the spirits for giving them a good day's hunting. Dances are also believed to help heal sick people. The San sing songs which remember their ancestors and ask the spirits for rain. It's a peaceful end to a long and tiring day. Now I'm really ready for my bed. I could sleep anywhere but I'm given a space on the ground behind a simple wall woven from dried grass. Each of the San has their own space. It's dry and out of the wind. Goodnight.

Next day
Up at dawn. It's time for the San to pack up their few belongings and set off for another campsite. They can't stay in one place for more than a few days. There's simply not enough food or water. And it's time for me to say goodbye.

I've had a brilliant time with the San. They're very kind and hospitable people, even though their lives are horribly hard. After even one day, I don't know how they keep going. I'll never complain about anything again.

NOTES:
The San have lived in the desert for 30,000 years. But now their lives are changing. Many have been badly treated and are being forced to leave their land. They're being made to settle down in shanty towns instead. It's a dreadful thing to happen to them. Some San are desperately fighting back to save their homes and their ancient culture. Otherwise they and their traditional desert skills may die out for ever. And that would be a terrible tragedy.

Teacher teaser

If you want to see your teacher really lost for words, forget Latin or ancient Greek. To confuse them utterly, speak Click. Start off with the word, "//kx'a". Helpful hint: to speak Click, it helps if you're good at pulling faces. Ready? First, pull your tongue quickly away from the sides of your mouth as if you're calling a horse. Then make a noise halfway between "k" and "g". Now make a little strangled sound as if you're choking. (Don't really choke.) Then finish off with an "aaahhh". Got all that? If you don't mind scaring yourself to death, try practising in a mirror.

But what are you trying to say?

Answer: Click is the language spoken by the San. In Click, "//kx'a" is the word for a type of tree. Click is horribly difficult to speak or understand, and can take years and years to master properly. And watch out. Even the tiniest little mistake can change a word's meaning utterly.

Desperate desert fact file

NAME: Kalahari Desert

LOCATION: Southern Africa

SIZE: 520,000,000 sq km

TEMPERATURE: Hot summers up to 49°C; cool winters with temperatures below freezing

RAINFALL: 130–460 mm

DESERT TYPE: High pressure and inland

DESERT DATA:

• It's mostly covered by ancient sand seas and dunes which formed over 10,000 years ago.

• It's home to the bizarre baobab tree which stores water in its trunk. When it's full it can measure 30 metres around its middle.

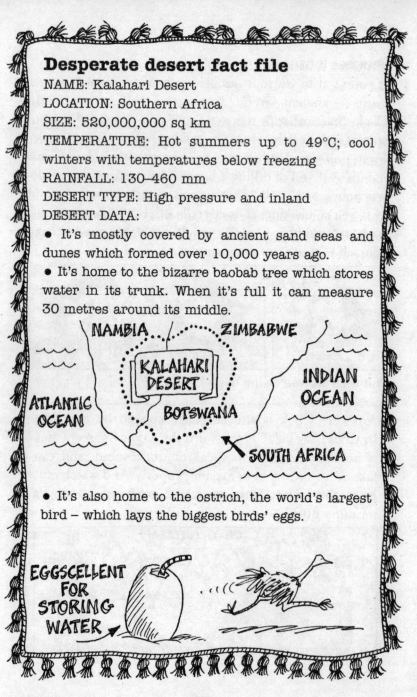

NAMBIA / ZIMBABWE

KALAHARI DESERT

ATLANTIC OCEAN

INDIAN OCEAN

BOTSWANA

SOUTH AFRICA

• It's also home to the ostrich, the world's largest bird – which lays the biggest birds' eggs.

EGGSCELLENT FOR STORING WATER

Finding a roof for the night

Many desert people are nomads. This means that they're constantly moving from place to place in search of food and water. They don't stay anywhere for long, just until supplies run out. Moving home all the time can get very tiring. In the desert, you can't just move from one ready-built house to another. There simply aren't any around. You have to carry your own home with you. So you need something that's quick to put up and take down, and that can be easily plonked on the back of your camel. Any ideas? What about a take-away desert tent?

Camping supplies catalogue

In a dilemma about which tent to choose? Don't worry. Our tents are specially designed to take the strain. Developed with the help of local desert people worldwide, they're ideal for camping out on the sand. We're proud to present our latest top-selling tent range...

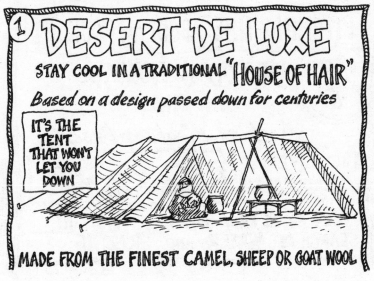

① DESERT DE LUXE

STAY COOL IN A TRADITIONAL "HOUSE OF HAIR"

Based on a design passed down for centuries

IT'S THE TENT THAT WON'T LET YOU DOWN

MADE FROM THE FINEST CAMEL, SHEEP OR GOAT WOOL

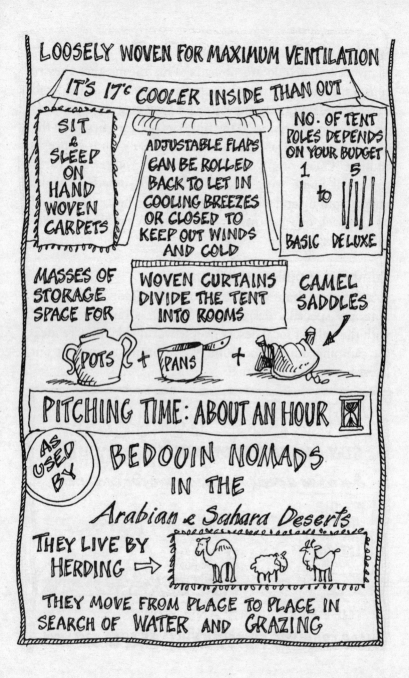

LOOSELY WOVEN FOR MAXIMUM VENTILATION

IT'S 17°c COOLER INSIDE THAN OUT

SIT & SLEEP ON HAND WOVEN CARPETS

ADJUSTABLE FLAPS CAN BE ROLLED BACK TO LET IN COOLING BREEZES OR CLOSED TO KEEP OUT WINDS AND COLD

NO. OF TENT POLES DEPENDS ON YOUR BUDGET

1 to 5

BASIC   DELUXE

MASSES OF STORAGE SPACE FOR

WOVEN CURTAINS DIVIDE THE TENT INTO ROOMS

CAMEL SADDLES

POTS + PANS +

PITCHING TIME: ABOUT AN HOUR

AS USED BY

BEDOUIN NOMADS IN THE

Arabian & Sahara Deserts

THEY LIVE BY HERDING →

THEY MOVE FROM PLACE TO PLACE IN SEARCH OF WATER AND GRAZING

Snug as a bug

FOR THOSE CHILLY DESERT NIGHTS. CHOOSE A TENT THAT REALLY KEEPS OUT THE COLD...

MONGOLIAN GER

HOLE IN ROOF TO LET SMOKE OUT

FOLD-UP WOODEN FRAME FOR EASY TRANSPORTATION

COMPLETE WITH ITS OWN COOKING FIRE

MADE FROM WARM SHEEP'S WOOL AND FELT

LIGHTWEIGHT AND EASY TO DISMANTLE

STAY WARM IN WINTER AND COOL IN SUMMER

PITCHING TIME: 30 MINUTES

AS USED BY **MONGOL** NOMADS IN THE GOBI DESERT

THEY HERD SHEEP AND GOATS, MOVING ABOUT TEN TIMES A YEAR

Two-Season Tents

TWO TRADITIONAL TENTS TO CHOOSE FROM. MADE FROM LOCALLY AVAILABLE MATERIALS. BOTH EASILY PACKED UP AND PORTABLE

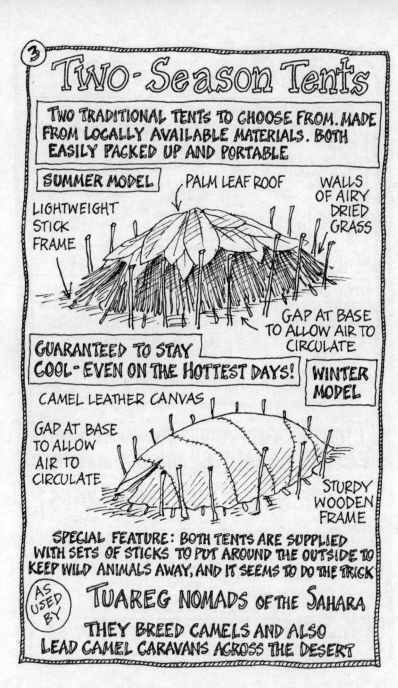

SUMMER MODEL

PALM LEAF ROOF

WALLS OF AIRY DRIED GRASS

LIGHTWEIGHT STICK FRAME

GAP AT BASE TO ALLOW AIR TO CIRCULATE

GUARANTEED TO STAY COOL - EVEN ON THE HOTTEST DAYS!

WINTER MODEL

CAMEL LEATHER CANVAS

GAP AT BASE TO ALLOW AIR TO CIRCULATE

STURDY WOODEN FRAME

SPECIAL FEATURE: BOTH TENTS ARE SUPPLIED WITH SETS OF STICKS TO PUT AROUND THE OUTSIDE TO KEEP WILD ANIMALS AWAY, AND IT SEEMS TO DO THE TRICK

AS USED BY TUAREG NOMADS OF THE SAHARA

THEY BREED CAMELS AND ALSO LEAD CAMEL CARAVANS ACROSS THE DESERT

THE QUICK-FIX SHELTER

IF YOU ONLY NEED OVERNIGHT ACCOMMODATION

FORGET STURDY GERS AND HOUSES OF HAIR

CHECK OUT THIS FLIMSY BUT FOOL-PROOF, NO FRILLS WINDBREAK

IT ONLY TAKES MINUTES TO BUILD

WALLS OF WOVEN GRASS

SIMPLE TWIG FRAME

PITCHING TIME: 10 MINUTES

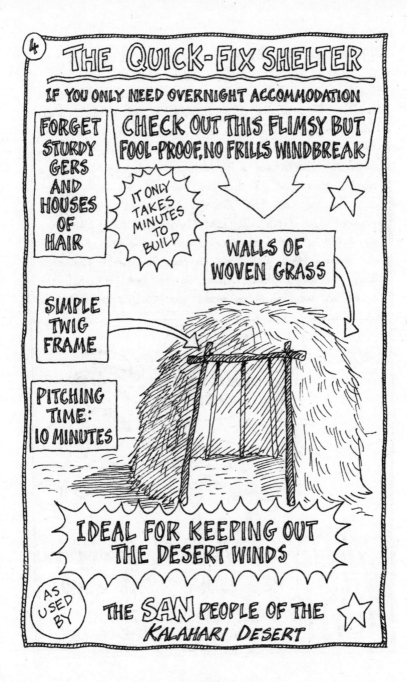

IDEAL FOR KEEPING OUT THE DESERT WINDS

AS USED BY

THE **SAN** PEOPLE OF THE *KALAHARI DESERT*

Dressed for the desert

Sandy here again, with a word of warning. If you're heading off into the desperate desert, you need to dress for the part. So what's the latest in desert fashion? Well, for a start, practicality's more important than style. So shorts and a T-shirt won't do, I'm afraid, no matter how good you look in them. Forget looking cool. It's keeping cool that counts. You need clothes that'll protect you from the sand, wind and sun. Otherwise you'll end up burnt to a crisp and looking like a dried-up old prune. (And just how un-cool is that!) The best thing to do, I always think, is to look at what the locals are wearing. Then model your clothes on theirs:

The Tuareg certainly know how to dress. And how to stay cool as a cucumber. So what's the secret of their success?

VERY NICE

MODEL NO 1: TUAREG NOMAD
OUTFIT: TRADITIONAL DRESS
SCORE: 10/10 (AN OLD DESERT HAND)

TURBAN: WOUND AROUND HIS HEAD AND NECK TO STOP SUNBURN

LOOSE-FLOWING ROBES: NOT ONLY PROTECT HIM FROM THE SUN BUT ALLOW COOL AIR TO CIRCULATE INSIDE

BLUE VEIL: COVERS HIS FACE AND MOUTH TO KEEP OUT SAND, DUST AND EVIL SPIRITS. TUAREG VEILS ARE DYED DEEP BLUE. (AND ONLY MEN WEAR THEM.)

LONG COTTON ROBES: TO PROTECT HIS WHOLE BODY

LEATHER SANDALS: FOR WALKING ACROSS HOT SAND

I've modelled my outfit on the Tuareg's. After all, it works for them. Personally, I think it looks really cool.

MODEL NO 2: SANDY
OUTFIT: TRENDY EXPLORER
SCORE: 8/10 (NOT BAD, THOUGH I SAY IT MYSELF!)

SUN HAT: ESSENTIAL, WIDE-BRIMMED IS BEST

SUNGLASSES: TO PROTECT YOUR EYES FROM THE GLARE

SCARF: FOR COVERING YOUR MOUTH AND NECK

BLANKET OR JUMPER: FOR THOSE COLD DESERT NIGHTS

STURDY BOOTS: MIND YOUR FEET DON'T GET BURNT

SHOW OFF!

LOOSE, LONG-SLEEVED SHIRT AND LONG BAGGY TROUSERS: FOR COOLNESS, COTTON'S BEST

Here's an example of how not to dress for exploring the desperate desert. Don't geography teachers know anything?

MODEL NO 3: MR TOMPKINSON
OUTFIT: GEOGRAPHY TEACHER
SCORE: 3/10 (DESPERATE! A REAL FASHION VICTIM.)

THINNING HAIR: WHERE'S THAT HAT?

TWEED JACKET: A BIT WORN AT THE ELBOWS

SHIRT AND TIE: FOR GETTING HOT UNDER THE COLLAR

BROWN, SUEDE SHOES: THAT HOLE WILL SOON BE LETTING IN SAND

Tea-time desert style

Now that you've got the clothes, it's time to meet the locals. Generally speaking, desert people are very hospitable. Even if they've never met you before, they'll offer you food and a place to stay. (Of course, once they get to know you better, it might be a different story!) So, it's important not to upset or offend them. (In the desert, you need all the friends you can get.) Here's a quick, step-by-step guide to minding your manners if a Tuareg invites you in for a cup of tea.

Are you brave enough to take tea with a Tuareg?

1 You arrive in a Tuareg camp. Act casual but be polite. Say "How do you do?" and shake hands with everyone, as if you've got all the time in the world. The Tuareg don't like to be hurried.

2 You're offered a glass of sweet mint tea. Drink it quickly and make lots of slurping noises. (This shows you're enjoying it.)

3 You're offered another glass of tea, then another. (By the way, it's very rude to refuse.) If it stops at three, congratulations. It means you're welcome to stay.

4 If you're given another glass (your fourth), you're welcome but not that welcome. Time to be on your way. Drink your tea, then get up, say your goodbyes (slowly, mind), and go.

Settling down

Not all desert people are nomads like the Tuareg. I mean, would you fancy moving house all the time? If you like the desert so much you can't bear to leave, why not pick a nice shady spot and settle down? You'll need water, of course, for drinking and growing your crops. But this is the desert so where can you find it? Well, the surface of the desert may look dusty and dry but there are buckets (and I mean buckets) of water under the sun-baked ground. You just need to know where to look for it.

Getting it out can be tricky, though. You could dig a well (you'll need to dig deep). Or you could sit and wait for the water to seep to the surface of its own accord and create a fabulously fertile ... oasis. (You might be waiting for a very long time – it could take 10,000 years for the water to surface.) Here's the inside story of how a flourishing oasis is formed.

1 Rain falls on the ground (it may be miles away) and soaks into tiny holes in the rock. This is called an aquifer. It's like a giant, rocky sponge. (Not great for using in the bath.)

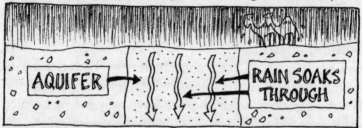

2 The water seeps along happily underground...

3 ...until it comes to a split in the rocks and can't go any further. Then it's forced to the surface.

4 Welcome to an oasis!

How green-fingered are you? With all that water lying around, you can grow loads of lovely fruit and veg. Like apricots, wheat and grapes, for a start. And palm trees... You might not think it to look at them but palm trees are horribly hardy and useful. You can eat their fruit (dates) raw, cooked or dried (like the ones you get at Christmas). You can use their trunks for building, their leaves for baskets and their seeds for camel food. And how about a tasty palm-bud salad? Delicious!

> *Horrible Health Warning*
>
> *But before you get too comfy and settled, remember that the desert can play tricks on your eyes. Tricks that can drive you mad with thirst. Picture the scene. You've run out of water and you're desperate for a drink. Just then, you spot an oasis ahead of you. Phew! You're saved. You think. But however fast you walk towards it, it just gets further and further away. That's because the oasis doesn't really exist. It isn't actually there. It's a mirage. And it's maddening.*

What happens is this:

1 A layer of warm air lies next to the ground.
2 It's trapped by a layer of cool air above it.
3 The layers bend the light coming from the sky.
4 So you think you see a refreshing pool of water rippling on the horizon. Lovely! But it's actually a reflection of the sky. (Worse still, it looks like it's fringed with shady palm trees. Sorry, more tricks of the light.)

Can you spot the difference?

Desperate desert survival quiz

Congratulations! You've come this far and you're still alive. You're really getting the hang of this desert-living lark. But what about your geography teacher? If he was stranded in the deserted desert, would he be able to survive? Or would his sense of adventure completely desert him? Try this deadly quiz on him to find out. All the answers are based on what local desert people would do in these situations. And they should know. After all, they've been surviving in the deadly desert since before your teacher was even born. And that's a very long time indeed!

1 You're in the Australian Desert and you're thirsty. Trouble is, there's no water for miles around. Just then, you hear a frog croaking. The sound seems to be coming from under the ground.

Do you bother to go and look for the frog? Yes/No

2 A diabolical dust storm is brewing in the Sahara Desert. You haven't got time to run for shelter so you decide to stand your ground and brave it out until the storm blows over.

Are you doing the right thing? Yes/No

3 You're in the Kalahari Desert with a group of San hunters. You're tracking an antelope when you spot a lion lurking in the bushes near by. You don't want to shout out a warning or the lion might hear you and charge.

San hunters have a range of hand signals to use in just this situation. Is this the right hand signal to use? Yes/No

4 You're looking for somewhere to pitch your tent and you spot a river valley (a *wadi*). It looks nice and level, and sheltered from the wind.

But is it really a safe place to camp? Yes/No

5 Your camel's playing up something rotten and you ask a local Bedouin camel herder for help. He tells you to pour spit down your camel's nose. But your camel's got a terrible temper and goodness knows what it'll do to you if you try.

Do you dare to follow the Bedouin's advice? Yes/No

6 The worst thing that could happen has happened. You've run out of water and you've still got miles and miles to go. You come across a Tuareg camp and stop to ask for supplies. You've learnt a bit of the local language and decide to try it out. Which word do you use for water? Would 'amise' do the trick? Yes/No

7 Oh dear, you're not having a very good day. You're out of suncream and your delicate skin is starting to burn. It'll be days before you reach a town where you can stock up on supplies. What can you use instead?

Would rubbing your skin with a watermelon work? Yes/No

Answers:

1 Yes. (Skip this next bit if you're squeamish.) This frog might save your life. It survives dry spells by storing water in its skin and sitting it out underground. Local Aborigines trick the frogs into croaking by stamping their feet on the ground. The stamping sounds to the frog like thunder which might mean rain!

Then the Aborigines dig the frogs up, hold them over their mouths and squeeeeeeze!

2 No. The best thing to do in a dust or sandstorm is crouch down next to your camel and cover your face and mouth. That's where a Tuareg veil comes in handy. If you stand up and try to brave it out, you'll be blown away or end up having stinging sand kicked in your face. Painful.

3 No. That's the signal for a duck, silly. And ducks don't scare anybody. By the time you've realized your mistake, it could be too late. The lion will have had you for lunch. Here's the signal you should have used.

DUCK   LION   CAR DOOR

4 No. Learn a lesson from the locals and never pitch your tent in a *wadi*. Whatever you do. It might look very inviting at the moment but all that could change if it starts to rain. One minute, the *wadi*'s nice and dry, the next it's a raging torrent. Flash floods can happen at any time and the ground simply can't soak up the overflow. So it pours down the *wadi*. You won't have time to call for help. You'll already have been swept away.

5 Yes. Your camel's probably been plagued by evil spirits. And the ancient Bedouin cure for this is to pour a mixture of water and camel spit down its nose. It's guaranteed to turn your camel into … a … er pussycat. But mind your camel doesn't try to bite you. I mean, how would you like having spit poured down your nose?

6 No. You'll have to try again. In the Tuareg language "amise" means camel. The word for water is "aman". But make sure you've got something to give the Tuareg in return for the water. Never go empty-handed. Sugar cubes always go down well (for making Tuareg tea, of course).

7 Yes. Believe it or not, it will work nicely. Instead of suncream, the San crush up some roasted watermelon seeds and mash them into a pulp. It's brilliant at protecting their skin from the sun. Of course, it might also make you irresistible to insects, especially if they've got a sweet tooth…

Now add up your teacher's score…

He gets one point for each right answer. How did he do?

Score: 0-2. Oh dear! Your teacher's brain seems to have wilted in the heat. His common sense seems to have utterly deserted him.

Score: 3-5. Not bad! Your teacher has kept his wits about him and not got too bogged down in the sand. But that looks like a nasty camel bite. How on Earth did he get it?

Score: 6-7. Congratulations! Your teacher's survived! (Now don't all cheer at once!) Why not enter him in the next Mr Desert Competition? It's held every year in the Thar Desert, India. He'll need to do well in five categories: moustache-growing (the longer and curlier, the better),

turban-tying (against the clock),

public speaking (last year's winning speech was called "Why I like the desert so much", cringe),

camel-racing (over 500 metres) and, finally, camel fancy dress.

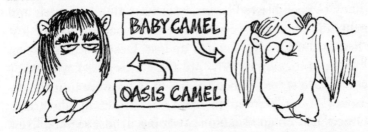

BABY CAMEL

OASIS CAMEL

Do you think your teacher has got what it takes to win the Mr Desert crown?

So, armed with loads of local knowledge, you've packed your teacher off to the desperate desert and you're looking forward to a few days off. Don't worry, he'll be following in well-trodden footsteps. Not only have local people lived in deserts for centuries, hundreds of intrepid explorers have also set off to find out what all the fuss was about. Some have even lived to tell the tale. (Some have never been seen again.) For others, though, it was a case of out of the frying pan and into the fire. If you get my drift...

DARING DESERT JOURNEYS

People have been exploring the deserts for centuries. They've been blasted by sandstorms, bitten by camels and generally fried alive. Some have gone mad, or bad or lost their cool. Many have ended up lost. Dead lost. So why on Earth did they do it? Why put their lives at risk when they could have stayed in bed? Some of them were in it for the money. They wanted to open the desert up for trade. Others had no good reason for going. It just seemed like a good idea at the time. An adventure of a lifetime. They had no idea what lay in store. Some, like your teacher, studied how the local people coped and copied their age-old desert skills. Which greatly improved their chances of survival. Fancy a horrible holiday?

Horrible Holidays are proud to present their

SENSATIONAL SAHARAN SAFARI

Fed up with ordinary caravan holidays?

1000 KM TO NOWHERE

Tired of squabbles about who gets the best bunk?

Had enough of sitting indoors in the rain?

BOOK YOUR PLACE TODAY

For a caravan holiday with a difference, book now on our deadly desert tour. (Better still, get your parents to pay.) Wave goodbye to crowded caravan sites, damp fields and traffic jams. Forget all about being squashed in a small space and those irritating cupboards that never stay shut. Time to get away from it all. Sleep under the stars in a luxury tent and soak up the age-old atmosphere of dreamy Timbuktu. It's the holiday that'll bring out the nomad in you.

Maximum 100 camels per caravan. (In the past, camel caravans travelling through the Sahara have been up to 1,800 strong).

HOW DO I SLEEP ON ONE OF THESE?

Led by expert Tuareg guides. (They've been leading camel caravans across the Sahara for hundreds of years.)

Tried and tested transport. (Caravans have been used for centuries to carry people and goods across the Sahara. The goods included dates, salt and gold which were carried to market to trade. The people included local traders and intrepid explorers – remember René Caillié? – who came along for the ride.)

What one satisfied customer said:
"It was brilliant. I got on really well with my camel. It only bit me once or twice. I'll never go in an ordinary caravan ever again."

Small print: Our caravans are hand-picked for your comfort. But you won't find mod cons like hot showers, central heating or tellies on board. If you can't live without them, we suggest you try our brand-new Couch Potato Tour. Coming soon to a sofa near you.

Desperate desert fact file

NAME: Australian Desert
LOCATION: Australia
SIZE: 3,800,000 sq km
TEMPERATURE: Hot summers up to 53°C; cold winters down to −4°C
RAINFALL: Less than 100 mm a year
DESERT TYPE: High pressure; rain shadow
DESERT DATA:

• Two-thirds of Australia is desperate desert.
• This is made up of the Simpson, Great Sandy, Great Victoria and Tanami deserts.
• Uluru is a huge red rock worn away by the desert wind. It's sacred to the Aborigine people.
• The largest desert lake is Lake Eyre. It filled for the first time on record in 1950.

or disappeared). And in 1795, they found the perfect volunteer – a keen, young Scottish doctor called Mungo Park (1771–1806). His mission was to track the river along its entire length from source to mouth. But first he had to find it. And that was easier said than done. Over the page is how Mungo might have described his journey in his letters to his boss, Henry Beaufoy…

Raging river fact file

NAME: River Niger

LOCATION: West Africa

LENGTH: 4,200 km

SOURCE: A deep ravine in the Fouta Djallon Highlands, Guinea

DRAINS: 188,340,000 sq km

MOUTH: Flows into the sea at the Gulf of Guinea in Nigeria.

FLOW FACTS:

• It's the third longest river in Africa, after the Nile and the Congo.

• Stocks of oil and gas have been found at its delta.

• The Niger's name comes from the African word 'n'ger-n-gereo' which means great river.

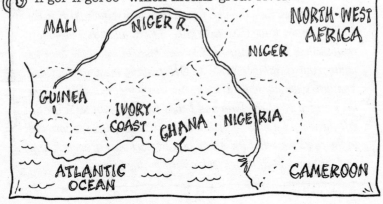

113

Nightmare on the Niger

A village in Africa, 30 March 1796

Dear Mr Beaufoy,

Thank you for your letter and the pay rise (yippee!). Fifteen shillings a day is really most generous. And it's come in the nick of time (but more of that later).

I don't know where on earth to begin to tell you all my news. The journey from England was most pleasant. The ship was adequate, the weather fair and the crossing took just 30 days. On landing in Africa, I headed down the River Gambia, according to plan, then continued by horse overland. (I must say, I am still rather saddlesore.)

For days we rode through flat, rolling grassland which made me pine for my beloved Scottish hills. The weather was also most troublesome. I was boiling hot by day and chilled to the bone by night. And it rained NON-STOP. I spent most of the time completely wet through. You see, my trusty umbrella had caught the eye of a local chieftain and I was forced to part with it as a gift (he wasn't a man to say no to). Still, I was looking forward to the challenges that lay ahead and to reaching my goal. Then, on Christmas Day, things took a turn for the worse.

A murderous mob of bandits attacked us and stole almost everything we owned. Right down to my waistcoat buttons! And in broad daylight! Then, to cap it all, I was arrested as a spy. Me! I've never spied on anyone in my life. I tried to talk my way out of it (you know how I pride myself on talking things through) but I ended up being clapped in the local prison.

Well, I somehow managed to give the guards the slip and make my escape but by now I had nothing but the clothes I stood up in. I was in very dire straits indeed. I don't know what would have become of me if a kindly old woman hadn't given me food though she hardly had enough for herself. (So you see, the pay rise really will come in handy.)

Luckily, the robbers didn't get their thieving fingers on my precious papers which I always keep safely tucked under my hat. You'll be pleased to hear that I've taken a great many notes about local customs (with a special chapter on prisons) which I look forward to showing you on my return. If I ever return... Until then, I shall press on with my quest.

Yours sincerely,
Mungo Park

Segon, on the Niger, Mali, 20 July 1796

Dear Mr Beaufoy,

   We've found it! We've found it! And it flows eastwards, not westwards as everyone thought. How it lifted my spirits to see it glistening there in the morning sun like the good old Thames at Westminster... It's BRILLIANT! I'm sooo excited. Yippeee!

   Bye for now,
   Mungo Park

PS Erm, sorry. I got a bit carried away. Very embarrassing and unscientific of me. I can promise you it won't happen again.

Somewhere up the Niger, 30 July 1796

Dear Mr Beaufoy,

   That's it – I've had it. I can't carry on. I'm tired, wet, penniless and my poor old horse is a gibbering wreck.

   I tried, I really tried. But enough is enough. You see, I hadn't the money for a canoe (I was robbed again – bang goes my pay rise) so, more dead than alive, my horse and I set off upstream to find the river's mouth. But it's been ten days now, and there's no end in sight. I asked a local chap if he knew where the river flowed to. He replied rather gloomily, "To the ends of the Earth." I can well believe it.

   Yours dejectedly, Mungo Park

Exhausted, broke and bitterly disappointed, Mungo Park went home. He still had nightmares about prisons but things very quickly looked up. He wrote a best-selling book of his travels and became a household name. (Well, would you forget a name like Mungo?) And while he was back home, he met and married the lovely Alison and settled down in Scotland to live happily ever after. Actually it was only for a little while. Despite everything, Mungo couldn't get Africa out of his mind. When he was offered another nose at the Niger, he was off like a shot. But he still found time to write to his wife...

Somewhere in West Africa, 13 June 1805

My Dearest Allie,

Half way through our journey now and things are going OK-ish, I suppose. Who am I kidding? It's been a disaster. Talk about leaving things to the last minute. It's been one delay after the other. First the soldiers sent to accompany me didn't show up (and when they did, they were a horribly bad-tempered, rowdy lot), then the supplies went missing.

Anyway, we finally set off. I know what you're thinking, dear. The rainy season's about to begin, I must be mad to go anywhere. But what choice did I have? If we'd waited any longer, we'd never have gone at all. And the sooner we get there, the sooner we can all go home...

Missing you dreadfully. Please don't worry. I'll be fine.

Your devoted Mungo

Sansanding, on the Niger, 17 November 1805

My dearest Allie,

    We finally reached the Niger on 19 August. I'm sorry I didn't write sooner but I've been rather busy with other things. To tell you the truth, things have been going from bad to worse. The rains made the going very soggy and slow (I know, you told me so) and very few of the men made it. I suppose a more sensible chap would have given up and gone home by now. But you know me, dear. Once I make up my mind to do something, I like to see it through to the bitter end. Call me a stubborn old fool, if you like.

    Things looked up a bit when the local chieftain promised me a couple of canoes. But they turned out to be rotten and full of holes.

    I saved what I could of the good wood and patched it together to make a boat. It's a bit leaky but it'll have to do. And now we're heading downstream. So you see, dear, the end is really and truly in sight.

    Dearest, I'm sending this letter by courier which should be quicker than boat. But I should be home long before it reaches you.

    Wish you were here, or I was there.

All my love,
Your Mungo

A watery end

If you only like stories with a happy ending, skip the next bit. This was Mungo's last letter to his wife. He was never heard from again. Only his local guide was left to fill in the gaps. According to him, Mungo sailed 2,400 kilometres down-river, fighting off enemy canoes and nosy hippos. Another 960 kilometres and he'd have reached the river's mouth and his journey's end. Then disaster struck. Mungo was ambushed by unfriendly locals. The game was up. Rather than wait to be killed, Mungo jumped into the river and was swept away.

Did he drown? Most people think so. But not everyone. For years, rumours reached Britain of a tall, red-headed man, speaking English, and living by the Niger...

As for the Africa Association who got poor Mungo into this mess in the first place, they were taken over by the British government. But this didn't stop them. They sent several more expeditions to follow in Mungo Park's footsteps. In 1830, the two Clapperton brothers set off up the Niger. People sniggered because of the way they dressed, in scarlet tunics, huge baggy trousers and enormous straw hats the size of umbrellas, but the Clappertons had the last laugh. Despite their critics, they managed to sail right down the river, right to its mouth and so finally put the River Niger well and truly on the map (though they only got a £100 reward for their pains).

River diseases

1 Malaria

Symptoms: Raging fever with a horribly high temperature. Terrible headaches, sweating and death. Especially bad in hot, swampy places.

Cause: Malarial mosquitoes which lay their eggs on the surface of slow-flowing rivers or ponds. When they hatch, they hover near the water. When they're hungry, they bite you, suck your blood and squirt deadly parasites into your veins. A parasite is a blood-thirsty creature that lives off other creatures. Nasty.

Any known cure? A course of pills usually does the trick. And of course it helps if you don't get bitten in the first place. Use mosquito repellant, cover up (particularly at dusk) and sleep under a mosquito net. An old-fashioned explorer's cure is to slap mud on your face! Well, it should take your mind off things!

2 River blindness

Symptoms: Horribly itchy skin. Damaged eyesight and in the worst cases blindness.

Cause: Blackflies which live and breed in tropical rivers. They bite you and spit tiny grubs into the wound.

Inside you, these grow into worms and lay their eggs which hatch into millions more worms. The worms spread through your body. Dead worms inside your eyes can make you go blind. Horrible.

Any known cure? A yearly dose of medicine, taken by mouth, can prevent blindness. Spraying rivers where blackflies breed helps to keep the disease at bay.

3 Bilharzia (bill-har-zi-a)

Symptoms: Itchy skin or rash, fever, chills, aches, pains and death. Can seriously damage your liver, guts, kidneys and bladder. So nothing too serious, then!

Cause: Tiny worm grubs. They live inside tropical river snails.

Then the grubs swap the snails for you. If you're in the river at the same time, the grubs can burrow through your skin and into your blood. There they lay their eggs. Yuck!

Any known cure? Yes, a simple injection or a course of pills.

Could you be a river rover?

Could you follow in Mungo Park's footsteps and become a raging river rover? Picture the scene... You've been walking for miles. You're tired, your feet hurt, you've been munched by what feels like a million mosquitoes and you just want to go home. You can see the path you need to take but, guess what? It's on the other side of a raging river!

So how on Earth do you get across? Decide which one of these methods you think would work best? Then check out the answers on pages 126–130.

1 Take a boat across it. Obvious really, but the question is what sort of boat do you choose? Take your pick from these raging river rovers.

A DUG-OUT CANOE

B FELUCCA

C JUNK

D STEAMBOAT

E FERRYBOAT

F CRUISESHIP

If you go by boat, watch out for sandbars. They're big dunes of sand on the river bed, ruffled up by the current. And they're horribly hazardous. The problem is they're so hard to spot and can suddenly shift without warning. Before you know it, you'll be grounded or even sunk. Best take a pilot with you (that's an expert in navigation). He'll know the river like the back of his hand.

2 Build a bridge across it. People have been bridging the gap for thousands of years. But what have bridges been made of? Which of these is too silly to be true?

a) old logs
b) old ropes
c) old rocks
d) old human heads

3 Dig a tunnel under it. Go on, get shovelling. It's not as silly as it sounds. There are several tunnels running under the River Thames in England. The first was built to last in 1842 by British engineer Marc Brunel. It was the first underwater tunnel in history. Today tube trains race through it.

4 Swim across it. If you're a strong swimmer, take a good, deep breath and dive in. But if your doggy paddle lets you down, you might need some help. If you can't be seen dead in armbands, hold on to a floating log for support. Or do what the ancient Assyrians did and grab on to a blown-up pig's bladder instead! Before you jump in, slap on plenty of insect repellant!

5 Pole vault over it. If all else fails, you could always go and take a running jump…

Answers:

1 All these boats can be used on rivers but it depends which river you choose. For fast-flowing rivers, dug-out canoes are just the job. They're light, tough and easy to steer. But watch out for particularly strong currents. Before you know it, you'll be swept downstream. To get over the river, paddle across and slightly upstream, HARD! For busy rivers, feluccas are neat and nippy for weaving in and out of traffic. They've been used on the Nile since Ancient Egyptian times. For deep, wide rivers, why not jump on a Chinese junk. Hope you're feeling strong. If the river's too high or too low, you might have to get out and pull. But if raging river currents are a problem, you'll need a boat with an engine. You could go for a modern motorboat but a classic old steamboat would really impress your friends. They were once a frequent sight on the Mississippi but now they mostly take tourists around. Fancy a bet? Some steamboats double up as floating casinos. For very wide rivers, hop on the ferry. Most big rivers have one. But get there early. They're often the only lift around and they can get horribly crowded. And finally, for rivers with history on their side, a cruiseship's the perfect choice. If you're feeling flash, why not cruise along the River Nile. You can see all the sights without leaving your deckchair.

2 d) Of course, you don't actually get bridges *built* of heads! Most of old London Bridge across the River Thames was made of sensible stone. But it also had a row of sharp spikes at each end. And guess what was on the ends of the spikes – yes, the chopped-off heads of traitors and criminals! Gruesome!

The very first bridges were probably logs or stepping stones laid across a stream. Rope bridges are often used in the jungle, made from vines. You have to hold on tight, as they wobble a lot.

Yes, bridges are often the quickest and easiest way of crossing a river. But you'll need to choose the right type. Are you brave enough to find out how to build a bridge?

What you need:
- some logs (assorted lengths)
- some stones
- a raging river

What you do:

a) Lay a long log across the river so it reaches from one bank to the other. Congratulations! You've made a simple beam bridge and it's great for crossing a narrow river.

GOOD DOG... GO AND FETCH THE FIRE BRIGADE...

b) For a wider river, you'll need a longer log and it needs to be stronger. Otherwise it will sag in the middle as you walk across it.

c) On a very wide river, you'll need to lay several logs end to end. Put a few piles of stones in the water for the logs to rest on. Technically, these piles are called piers.

RIVER

BEAM OF LOGS

PIERS: TOPS STICK JUST ABOVE THE WATER

Note: if the river's horribly deep and wide, forget beam bridges. The logs and piers would be just too huge. Instead you'll need a suspension bridge. That's a bridge which hangs from long, steel cables suspended from tall towers. These bridges can be more than a kilometre long. And that's a job for a proper engineer!

Horrible Health Warning

Messing about on rivers can be dangerous. Be careful that you don't slip and fall in. The water may be deeper than you think and there may be strong currents which could sweep you away.

3 Tunnelling can work but be careful. Even for experts, underwater tunnels are tricky to build. Because they go under the soft riverbed rocks, their roofs and walls can easily cave in. Brunel had to design a special tunnelling machine for the job. It burrowed through the rock, holding up the roof while the workers were left to line the tunnel. Clever, eh? Especially when you know that Brunel got the idea from watching a wood-boring mollusc at work. Modern tunnelling machines are still based on Brunel's brilliant invention.

4 This is a good idea, if you can swim, though maybe leave out the pig. And watch out for weirs. They're small, low dams built across the river and they block the river to make a deep pool like a small harbour for boats. They're often hidden by the water – making them doubly dangerous. If you're swept over one, you'll get sucked into the swirling water and you won't be able to get out again. They're just as dangerous if you're in a small boat.

5 Strangely enough, you'd be in good company. Believe it or not but this is how the sport of pole vaulting began with people using sticks to leap across streams. You should easily make it if the river's narrow but get a good run up if it's wide. Otherwise you're in for a horribly soggy landing.

So, which works best? Well, there's no real right or wrong answer to that because all raging rivers are different!

Earth-shattering fact
What if the river's too narrow or shallow to take big ships? You make it deeper and wider, of course! That's what engineers did to the St Lawrence River in North America. And they tacked some canals on the end. Ships can now make the 3,769-kilometre trip from the Atlantic Ocean and across the Great Lakes in just eight days. The only snag is that the waterway's blocked by ice in winter and there's nothing the engineers can do about that!

You might think that deadly diseases, life-threatening weirs and leaky canoes were the worst that the river could throw at you. But you'd be wrong, horribly wrong. So far, your river's been quite well behaved. It's true. But things are about to change. Prepare to be swept off your feet. You're about to see the other side of the river. A side you haven't seen before. When the river's true colours come flooding out...

RIVER RAGE

If you think things look bad when your teacher loses his temper, beware of a river in a rage. In a flash, a river can change completely from a nice, babbling brook to a raging torrent. If this happens to a river near you, get out of the way, fast! Furious floods can be horribly hazardous, sweeping away everything in their path. INCLUDING YOU! And the freaky thing is that they can happen anywhere, anytime…

What on Earth is a flood?

Want to find out about floods but too wet to ask? Worried about keeping your head above water? Here's Travis to throw you in at the deep end…

SO, WHAT ON EARTH IS A FLOOD THEN ?

It's when a raging river overflows because it's too full of water. Simple really. Like when you fill a glass too full of pop.

HMM, I SEE, AND WHY DOES THIS HAPPEN ?

Most floods happen when massive, and I mean massive, amounts of rain fall in a very short time. The river just can't cope. You also get floods when melting snow swells the river or when a dodgy dam bursts. Or when cyclones or tidal waves whip up the sea into a frenzy.

BLIMEY! WHERE DOES ALL THE OVERFLOW GO ?

It spills on to the floodplain. That's the flat land on either side of the river which is normally dry. It can be a few metres across or a few hundred kilometres, and it's made of mud and sand dumped by the river.

WHY DOESN'T THE WATER JUST SOAK INTO THE GROUND? THEN IT WOULDN'T MATTER IF THE RIVER FLOODED.

Good point. But it's not as simple as that, I'm sorry to say. If the rain's very heavy, the ground can't soak it up fast enough and the soil becomes water-logged. Then any floodwater just lies on top.

AND ARE FLOODS REALLY DANGEROUS?

Yes and no. Some rivers flood every year without doing much damage. But a really fierce flood can be fatal. It can drown fields and crops, wash away buildings and cause millions of pounds of damage. And cost lives. In fact, furious floods do more damage and kill more people than any other natural disaster. And that's official! The worst flood on record happened in 1931, when the Huang He River in China burst its banks killing no less than 4 million people and leaving 80 million homeless. Horrible.

WHY DON'T PEOPLE LIVE SOMEWHERE SAFER?

Millions of people don't have much choice. They live in countries where there's already too little land to go round. Besides, the soil on the floodplain is so fantastically fertile, they're willing to run the risk.

133

WHICH RIVERS SHOULD I AVOID AT ALL COSTS?

Most rivers can turn nasty if conditions are right. But without doubt one of riskiest is the raging Yangtze River in China...

The Daily Globe

Sunday 2 August 1998, Hunan Province, eastern China

MILLIONS IN FEAR AS FLOOD WATERS RISE

A week after the Yangtze burst its banks for the third time in two months, millions of Chinese are still on full flood alert. Today, water levels on the river broke all previous records, leaving terrified villagers in fear of being literally washed away.

The Yangtze has been rising since spring, placing enormous pressure on the fragile system of dykes or embankments which separate the river from the 200 million people living along its banks. With floodwater now surging downstream, people are getting really very frightened.

"We're praying we can prevent a disaster," an elderly villager told our reporter. "We've been making the dykes round our village higher with mud. But if the dykes don't hold when the river comes, we'll lose everything."

DAM BUILDERS

Elsewhere in the region some dykes have already collapsed and several villages lie swamped under two metres of water. This year's floods have already claimed 2,500 lives – numbers are still rising – and driven millions of villagers out of their homes. Some have been stranded for days on their roofs, helplessly watching the unstoppable rise of the water.

ROOF TOPS

And now a new danger is lurking. Doctors are warning that disease could be the next disaster to strike. In some places, polluted floodwater has already contaminated drinking water and placed millions at risk of sickness and diarrhoea.

But getting the sick to hospital is no easy matter.

"I saw some people being rowed to hospital in boats," an eyewitness said. "But the first floor of the hospital was under water. I don't know how they got in."

So, who is to blame for the disaster? This is a question many people are asking. True, the river has been flooding for centuries but this year's torrential summer rains have made the problem much worse. Some people blame the government for not spending enough money on repairing the dykes. If they don't act soon, locals fear, the same thing will happen again and again.

"I have nothing," one farmer told us after he'd seen his home, all his belongings and his crops completely washed away. "I'll have to start all over again."

And this may not be the last time…

Raging river fact file

NAME: Yangtze River

LOCATION: China

LENGTH: 6,418 km

SOURCE: Mount Gelandandong, Tibet

DRAINS: 1,683,500 sq km

MOUTH: Flows into the East China Sea (part of the Pacific Ocean) near Shanghai.

FLOW FACTS:

• In Chinese, it's called the Chang Jiang or Long River. Legend says it was carved out by a goddess.

• It's the world's third longest river after the Nile and Amazon.

• About three-quarters of all the rice grown in China is grown on its floodplain.

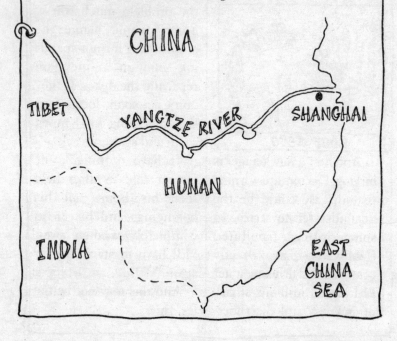

CHINA

TIBET

YANGTZE RIVER

SHANGHAI

HUNAN

INDIA

EAST CHINA SEA

The 1998 Yangtze flood was what horrible geographers call a 100-year flood. But what on Earth does this mean? Well, floods are rated by how often they might happen. The more frequent they are, the better. A one-year flood is likely to happen once a year and doesn't do much damage. A 100-year flood means that, each year, there's a one-in-a-hundred chance of a flood that can do a lot of damage. Making it horribly dangerous. Phew! If that sounds bad, imagine the horror of the people of Lynmouth, England, when a freak 50,000-year flood smashed their village to pieces in 1952.

At least there shouldn't be another flood like it (with that river, at any rate!) for a very, very long time.

Could you be a flood hydrologist?

Once a river's in full flood, there's nothing scientists can do to stop it. But they can try to find out where a flood will strike next. If they can work out when and where a flood's likely to happen, they can sound the alarm and get people out of the way. It isn't easy – floods are horribly fickle.

Do you have what it takes to be a flood hydrologist? (That's the posh title for a horrible scientist who studies floods.)

HORRIBLE JOB ADVERT

Tired of keeping your feet on the ground?
Is life driving you round the bend? Fancy
a spell in the fast stream? Why not join
our team of top hydrologists?

- You must like the outdoors and be a
strong swimmer.

- You must be good at maths and making
graphs (especially flow charts).

- You mustn't mind getting your feet wet.

- Full training will be given.
Still interested? Why not meander along
to your local Careers Centre?

Raging rivers – the career you can bank on

And here's Travis to show you the ropes…

Travis's (almost) fool-proof guide to flood forecasting

1 Get to know your river

You need to study your river carefully and get to know all of its twists and turns. Most importantly, you need to see how it reacts when it rains. Ask yourself these two questions:

a) How much rain is falling? You don't need loads of posh measuring gear for this. You can make a simple rain gauge from a kitchen measuring jug.

But serious scientists also scan the skies for rain using high-tech radars and weather satellites.

b) How much is the river rising? Scientists study river levels with a nifty gadget called a stream sensor. It radios back data to a computer.

c) Some hot-shot hydrologists go a step further and build their own model river, complete with fake meanders, floodplains and floods. They use this to test how the river reacts and how dams and dykes hold up against floods.

FLASH FLOOD!

2 Chart your river's progress

Next, feed all your info into a computer. It will do loads of earth-shattering equations and plot the results on a chart. (The posh name for this is a hydrograph.) But you'll need to double check it's got things right and that's where being wicked at maths will help. The chart will show how the river copes with rain, and how long before it overflows. From this you can work out how likely a flood is and how long you've got to get outta there...

3 Sound the alarm

If it's raining heavily and the river's rising rapidly, for goodness' sake sound the alarm! In Britain, flood warnings are colour-coded according to the degree of risk.

- **Yellow Warning**

  Risk of flooding to low-lying farmland and roads near rivers.

- **Amber Warning**

  Risk of flooding to isolated homes and larger areas of farmland near rivers.

- **Red Warning**

  Risk of serious flooding to many properties, roads and large areas of farmland.

So how watertight was your warning? Of course, you can't tell for sure until the flood's been and gone. The trouble is that floods are horribly unpredictable. You can't always work out what they'll do next. For big rivers like the Mississippi, you might have a week's warning of flooding. But you might have just a few hours to flee from a flash flood. (That's a flood that rises incredibly quickly after an unusually heavy downpour of rain.)

Stopping the flow

You know the saying, "Prevention is better than cure"? It means that it's better to stop your teeth rotting in the first place by not eating too many sweets than to spend hours afterwards at the dentist. It's usually used about people. But the same could be said for floods. You might not be able to stop a flood in mid-flow but you can take steps to reduce the damage. How? Well, for a start, you could…

• **Plant some trees.** Here's how it works:

1 Plant leaves trap rain before it can hit the ground. In a forest, about three-quarters of rain is waylaid like this.

2 Plant roots suck up water from the soil, and also bind the soil together.

The problem is that plants and trees are being cut down for firewood or to clear farmland. And this means there's nothing to stop the rain pouring into the river. The rain also washes away loads of loose soil which raises the river bed so it floods more easily.

• **Change the shape of the river.** Try making the river straighter, wider and deeper. It'll work wonders. It makes it easier for the river to flow so it reaches the sea faster without overflowing. But you'll need a special digging machine called a dredger.

• **Change the river's course.** By building a ditch or channel to divert the water away. It's also useful for storing spare water. These diverting ditches are called spillways.

• **Dam it.** Dams are horribly handy for flood control. But are they any good? Who better to ask than a couple of horrible hydrologists? The only problem is finding two hydrologists that agree. About anything! Take these two, for a start:

DAMS ARE BRILLIANT BECAUSE THEY STOP RIVERS FLOODING, AND WE KNOW HOW USEFUL THAT IS. AND THEY MAKE SURE THERE'S A STEADY SUPPLY OF WATER FOR DRINKING AND FARMING. AND THEY CAN GENERATE LOADS OF CHEAP CLEAN ELECTRICITY. WHAT MORE COULD YOU ASK?

DAM BUILDER

DAMS ARE DISASTROUS BECAUSE THEY FORCE MILLIONS OF PEOPLE OUT OF THEIR HOUSES AND DROWN THE LAND UNDER TONNES OF WATER. THEY ALSO WIPE OUT WILDLIFE. AND IF YOU WAVE GOODBYE TO FLOODS, IT'S BYE BYE FERTILE FLOOD-PLAINS AND DELTAS TOO. BESIDES DAMS COST A FORTUNE TO BUILD AND WHAT HAPPENS IF ONE GOES AND BURSTS?

DAM BUSTER

Talk about putting a spanner in the works! It's difficult to know just who to believe.

• **Build an embankment.** One of the oldest ways to stop a flood is to make the riverbank higher. You could do this by building a mud or concrete embankment, or dyke. But does this waterproofing work? The answer is; sometimes it does, and sometimes it doesn't. Along the Mississippi, embankments are called levees. (That's French for "raised".) There are thousands of kilometres of them along the river. For years, they've been the main flood-proofing measure. But what happens when a levee springs a leak? Then things go horribly wrong, as the terrible true story on the next page shows...

Raging river fact file

NAME: Mississippi River

LOCATION: USA

LENGTH: 3,780 km

SOURCE: Lake Itasca, Minnesota, USA

DRAINS: 3,256,000 sq km

MOUTH: Flows into the Gulf of Mexico (part of the Atlantic Ocean) at its huge delta.

FLOW FACTS:

• Its longest tributary, the Missouri, is actually 350 km longer than the Mississippi itself. The two rivers meet near St Louis.

• New Orleans is protected by several long levees. Which is just as well because the city lies below river level!

• Its nicknames include Old Man River and Big Muddy.

WHAT THEY SAID ABOUT IT: "You cannot tame that lawless stream." (Mark Twain)

After the Great Flood, summer 1993

For millions of people living along the Mississippi floods are a fact of life. But things seemed to be getting better. It had been 20 years since the last big flood and, with higher and stronger levees, backed up by new dams and spillways, floods seemed a thing of the past.

The new measures seemed to have done the trick. Or had they? True, it had been a very wet year with record-breaking rains. But the floods, if they came, usually happened in spring. By summer, the river was usually falling. What happened that summer took everyone by surprise.

With no break in the rain, the Mississippi became a raging torrent, flowing at six times its usual speed. In places, it rose seven metres above normal, a raging brown torrent of water and mud.

The new flood measures failed miserably. In the state of Illinois alone, 17 levees crumbled under the strain ... including the one protecting the little town of Valmeyer.

Local people worked round the clock, filling thousands of sandbags to fight back the flow. But despite their best efforts, they could not stop the wall of water that poured into the town.

Fortunately, the town had just been evacuated. Miraculously, only one person died and no one was seriously injured. Everyone knew that it could have been much worse.

Three weeks later, the townspeople were allowed to return home to start the massive clean-up. Valmeyer had been turned into a waterlogged ghost town. Windows were smashed, all the lights were out, and thick muddy sludge covered everything. The eerie quietness was broken only by the buzzing of huge swarms of mosquitoes.

"It's heartbreaking," one man said as he looked at the wreckage of his home. "I've lived here all my life and it's all gone. Everything's covered in mud and mould. But at least we've got each other and a disaster sure makes folk rally round." Only four houses were left standing. Others were water-filled wrecks. Their only occupants were frogs, crayfish and ... poisonous snakes. Everyone had to up sticks and start all over again. (And after a second soaking in September, that's exactly what happened. The whole town moved lock, stock and barrel, to higher, drier ground.)

The Great Flood of 1993 was America's worst natural disaster. The flood covered an area the size of England and seven states were declared disaster zones. The water caused $10 billion of damage, flooded 50 towns, destroyed 43,000 homes and left 70,000 people homeless. Millions of acres of crops were washed away. And only a quarter of the levees were left in one piece.

Earth-shattering fact
Imagine a busy city like London. Now imagine it under a metre of water... All it would take is a high tide surging up the River Thames from the sea. To stop such a disaster, a massive barrier was built across the Thames in 1984. When high tides are due, ten huge steel gates swing up from the river bed to make a gigantic dam. The barrier's already had to close more than 30 times...

Travis's top waterproof flood warnings

If building a dam is beyond you, or your homework doesn't leave you enough time, what on Earth can you do if a flood's flowing your way? Try to remember these basic Do's and Don'ts and you'll save yourself from a soaking:

DO...
- Stay tuned to your radio for flood warnings.

Or listen out for a siren, if time's short. Some countries run a telephone flood–warning service. If you can get to the phone...

- Switch off the gas and electricity. Water and electricity are an explosive mix. NEVER touch electrical equipment with wet hands. Ever. Water is a brilliant conductor of electricity which means that electricity can shoot through it very easily indeed. And it could give you a killer shock.

- Stock up on sandbags. If you're staying put, block up doorways and air bricks with sandbags. You can buy them or make your own from some strong cloth sacks and sand.

• Go upstairs. And take any other people, pets and valuables with you, out of reach of the water.

• Pack some supplies. Whether you're going or staying, you'll need emergency stores to tide you over for a few days. Pack warm clothes, blankets, food, water, a torch and some batteries. Stuff these in strong plastic bags ready to grab when you need them.

• Be prepared to leave home. If the flood's really serious, you may have to move fast. Head for higher ground away from the river. Better still, go to stay with some friends.

Once you're outside…
DON'T…

• Try to cross any floodwater by foot. If it reaches your ankles, turn back and find another route. The water may be deeper than it looks and the road underneath may have been washed away.

• Go for a drive. At least, not through flood water. It often flows fast enough to wash cars away. And cars can quickly turn into death-traps if you break down. By the time the water reaches the windows, the water pressure will be too strong for you to open the door. If you do have to drive, open the windows before you set off. That'll equalize the pressure inside and outside the car.

• Drink any floodwater. However thirsty you are. Floodwater's filthy, thanks to all the mud, debris and even sewage it sucks along. Ideal for germs to fester in. If you're staying at home, fill the bath with clean water, and boil any water you use.

• Camp near a river bed. Even if it looks dry. It could fill up in seconds and wash you away.

• Ever try to outrun the flood. However fast you run, it'll be right behind you...

You might think that spending your whole life studying water might turn a hydrologist's brain horribly soggy and soft. But these soaking scientists are not as wet as they seem.

They're working their socks off trying to forecast floods more accurately. The good news is that they're getting quicker at spotting the warning signs and moving people out of the way. The bad news is that forecasts can never be watertight. It can't be a cut and dried case. Why? Well, floods are just too horribly unpredictable.

REVOLTING RIVERS

Never mind messing about on rivers. After everything rivers have done for us, what are we doing in return? The sickening answer is making a mess of them. Horrible humans have made some rivers so disgustingly dirty, they've been declared officially DEAD! (The revolting rivers, not the humans. Though if your drinking water came from one of them, you might soon be a gonner too.) So why on Earth is freshwater so filthy? Why not...

Make your own rancid river soup

What you need:

- stinking sewage (it's usually treated in a sewage works before it's clean enough to be pumped into the river but in some places it goes in ... as it is!)
- filthy factory waste (this might be dirty water or poisonous metals and chemicals)
- fertilizers and pesticides (washed off farmers' fields)

What you do:

1 Chuck all the ingredients into a river and leave to fester.

2 Sprinkle a few bottles and tin cans on top.

3 Now offer a bowlful to your teacher!

Raging river fact file

NAME: River Ganges

LOCATION: India and Bangladesh

LENGTH: 2,510 km

SOURCE: Gangotri glacier, Himalayas

MOUTH: Flows into the Indian Ocean at the Bay of Bengal.

DRAINS: 975,900 sq km

FLOW FACTS:

• It joins the Brahmaputra River in Bangladesh and empties into the world's biggest delta.

• A huge mangrove swamp stretches along the delta. It's home to man-eating crocodiles and tigers.

• About half a billion people live on its floodplain.

Cleaning up the gungy Ganges

For millions of people living along the Ganges, the river doubles up as a water supply and a drain. They don't have the money for posh treatment plants, so every day, millions of litres of smelly sewage and killer chemicals are flushed straight into the river. And that's not all...

Many people believe that the river is holy and that bathing in its water will wash their sins away. People also come to the river to die. Their bodies are cremated (burnt), then their ashes are thrown into the water. Sometimes bodies are also thrown in. Animal and human bodies. It may sound morbid to you but for people in India it's very important. The problem is that it's not doing the river much good. Some of the Ganges is so horribly polluted that it's putting people's health at risk.

In 1985 things got so bad that a massive clean-up campaign began. Part of the plan was to build hundreds of new sewage treatment works. (Warning – you'll need a strong stomach for the next bit.) Another part of the plan was to flood the river with turtles. Yes, turtles. Meat-eating turtles who would munch up the dead. Gruesome but brilliant.

But has it worked? Is the gungy Ganges now gleaming with health? Well, not exactly; but it's certainly getting cleaner – though how much of that is down to the tasteless turtles, no one can really tell.

Earth-shattering fact
In 1858, the smell from the River Thames was so bad that it put MPs (Members of Parliament) in the nearby Houses of Parliament right off their work. They renamed the river the Great Stink. Thank goodness things have got a bit more fragrant.

Fragrant flowers

But it isn't all doom and gloom. The good news is that people are really trying to clean up their act. On many rivers, action plans are already up and running. Remember the reeking Rhine? For years it was known as the 'sewer of Europe'. Well, things are now looking up. The river was well-stocked with salmon until about 50 years ago. (Salmon are particularly sensitive to pollution.) The aim is to bring the salmon swimming back in the next few years. And there are strict rules to help it happen.

Which is great news for raging rivers all over the world. And for you. Before very long, you'll be back by the riverbank, a drink and a fishing rod in your hands, with not a horrible field trip in sight...

If you're still interested in finding out more, here are some websites you can visit:

http://www.amrivers.org/
North America's leading national river conservation organization

http://www.cis.umassd.edu/~gleung/
Yellow River, the longest river in China, has its own homepage!

http://www.amazonthefilm.com/
The official Amazon river website with photos, a quiz and even an Amazon movie!

HORRIBLE INDEX